D1527503

PEDAGOGY, DEMOCRACY, AND FEMINISM

SUNY Series, Teacher Empowerment and Reform
Henry A. Giroux and Peter L. McLaren, editors

PEDAGOGY, DEMOCRACY, AND FEMINISM

Rethinking the Public Sphere

Adriana Hernández

STATE UNIVERSITY OF NEW YORK PRESS

Published by
State University of New York Press, Albany

© 1997 State University of New York

For information, address the State University of New York Press,
State University Plaza, Albany, NY 12246

Production by Christine Lynch
Marketing by Fran Keneston

Library of Congress Cataloging-in-Publication Data

Hernandez, Adriana.
    Pedagogy, democracy, and feminism : rethinking the public sphere /
by Adriana Hernandez.
        p.   cm. — (SUNY Series, teacher empowerment and school
    reform)
    Includes bibliographical references (p.   ) and index.
    ISBN 0-7914-3169-X (hc : acid-free). — ISBN 0-7914-3170-3 (pb :
acid-free)
    1. Critical pedagogy. 2. Feminism and education. 3. Democracy.
I. Title. II. Series: Teacher empowerment and school reform.
LC196.H47 1997
370.11′5—dc20   96-1934
                                                                       CIP

10 9 8 7 6 5 4 3 2 1

CONTENTS

ACKNOWLEDGMENTS

I give thanks to Henry Giroux for nurturing me in the process of coming to voice and for guiding me in the articulation of my dissertation. I give special thanks to Susan Jarratt for her moral support, for thinking with me through the implications of the central positions in this work, and also for editing my text. I thank Richard Quantz for his constant intellectual advice and his friendship all along my journey in the USA. Thanks to Peter McLaren for his incredible generosity and for encouraging me to get a doctoral degree. I also want to thank Nelda Cambron-McCabe, the chairperson of the EDL department at Miami University, and Dennis Carlson for their support. Thanks to Guillermo Villanueva, the Dean of the School of Education at the University of Comahue (1986–1993), for making it possible for me to pursue graduate studies abroad and also for granting me the institutional time to further develop my doctoral dissertation into a book. Thanks to Susana Barco for her support and for advising me on the scholarship project. Thanks to Mechi Rosso, who registered me in the LASPAU-Fulbright program before I even had time to think about it. Thanks to the Mothers in Neuquén, Inés Ragni, Beba Mujica and Lolin Rigoni, for sharing with me their collective struggle.

FOREWORD

PETER L. McLAREN and HENRY A. GIROUX

This year both of us were fortunate to visit Argentina as invited guests of student and teacher organizations in Buenos Aires (Giroux), and in Rosario and Santa Fe (McLaren). Returning to Los Angeles from Rosario, the birthplace of Ernesto "Che" Guevara, after speaking at a conference in honor of El Che's birthday, McLaren found the contrasting political imagery to be staggering. Alarmingly distinct from the plethora of posters of the charismatic El Che, which festooned every nook and cranny of space housing the conference, was a *Los Angeles Times* photograph of Bob Dole at a Southland political rally. Dole's lifeless visage was in stark contrast to the spirited rhetoric of his speech: Anglos are being ripped-off in California by Latinoamericans—mostly Mexicanos and Mexicanas—and it is time that civilized folks wrestled the land back from the barbarians. Glancing further at the *Times*, it was obviously news as usual from the western front: churches serving Southern Blacks are being routinely razed; the border continues to be militarized; Klu Klux Klan leader Darrell Flinn, Imperial Wizard of the Knights of the White Kamellia of Lafayette, Louisiana, continues to be a popular talk show guest in the nation's media; militia and survivalist movements proliferate throughout the country as their members incant millenianist slogans calling for an apocalyptic showdown between "whites" and "non-whites"; copies of *Turner Diaries* continue to be snapped up by right-wing hate groups that foster a Manichean "us"-against-"them" mindset; and the Fangs of the Viper militia, of Phoenix, is dismantled by federal agents.

Bob Dole's speech had its usual "gaff"—in this one, he described the United States as a "boiling pot" of populations, rather than the now shopworn "melting pot." Ironically, "boiling pot" is a more accurate metaphor for ethnoracial relations in the United States, especially in light of the 1992 Los Angeles uprising, when eroding "structures" actually did "take to the streets"—largely as a result of (1) the government's steady retreat from both civil rights and urban reform, and (2) the current global restructuring of capitalism.

Many Argentine educators, wrestling with their own serious educational problems, look to Europe and the United States for leadership in the battle over curricular reform and the privatization of schools. At the same time, public education in the United States appears to be facing ever greater setbacks. It is alongside the eroding democratic possibilities for education, which accompany neoliberal economic and educational restructuring efforts in both the United States and Latinoamerica, that the transgressive reading by Argentine feminist Adriana Hernández, *Pedagogy, Democracy, and Feminism*, needs to be engaged. This work goes beyond an inaugural strategy or liberal installment of a democratic theory of schooling. Rather, it offers a radical counterpoint to the masculinist, racist, and neoliberal cant offered up by politicians as mammon for the people, a counterpoint that draws upon feminist theory and critical pedagogy from both U.S. and Latinoamerican contexts. Professor Hernández articulates a powerful conception of feminist pedagogy in which "pedagogy is at the interior of political, cultural, distributive, and appropriative practices in the sense of representing a strategy for the interrogation and transformation of knowledge, interest, desires, and subjectivities in a complex dialectical process." Hernández contests masculinist cultures in which norms, conventions, regulations, and systems of intelligibility can be characterized as repressive, hostile to, and exploitative of women. Culture is viewed as a contested reality among various possible collective meanings espoused by groups occupying differential arrangements of power relative to one another on the basis of class, ethnicity, and gender. Culture is conceived as a heterogeneity of interwoven discourses, in which certain masculinist privileges are sustained and reproduced.

For Hernández, a feminist pedagogy of difference must concern itself not only with the production of knowledge, but with the constitution of the subject and the production of subjectivities. Her pedagogical imperatives are grounded in the articulation and interpretation of student subjectivities. Influenced by Laclau and Mouffe's approach to the analysis of democracy and their acceptance of antagonism and conflict as inevitable, and taking seriously the notion put forward by Bowles and Gintis that "political, distributive, appropriative and cultural practices are all present at once in diverse sites," Hernández challenges the binary and oppositional relations in which concepts such as "private/public" and "us/them" are situated. She does not essentialize antagonism by locating men as the intransigent enemy of social justice. Rather, she attempts to overturn the hierarchical dualisms and the dichotomized, gendered subjectivity that produces men who are complicitous with sexism, racism, and homophobia, as well as capitalist patriarchal relationships of domination and exploitation.

Hernández argues that the excess and overlap of binary oppositions in public/private articulation speaks to the need to reconsider "public" and "private"—not as fixed essences, but rather as shifting relationships. Hernández has constructed a powerful feminist analysis that sets out to examine the relationships between subjective ways of knowing and objective, historical moments that frame experiences and social relations. Hernández recognizes the essential difference between a feminist and non-feminist articulation of agency and, as such, she locates experience as a legitimate and rich ground for feminist interpretation. According to Hernández, experience is never seamless or totalized, but is always open to being re-imagined within a broad socio-historical, geopolitical and cultural framework that underscores the complexity and situatedness of places, relationships, and practices.

Hernández considers subjectivity to be a nexus of possible futures where the personal and public remain unclosed constructions, and where conditions of impossibility become (paradoxically) the constituent ground for relations of possibility. Agency, in this view, is neither panhistorically undecidable nor metaphysically unassailable. Rather, it is used in the service of a critique of capitalist social relations.

Drawing on the work of Maria Lugones, Hernández argues that "what may be a powerful strategy for white women turns out to be a painful alienation for Hispanic ones." Hernández—who addresses the exclusionary textual and social practices that inform the subjectivities of Latinas in the United States, and, who, as a Third World woman, writes with the double awareness of being "self" and "other"—articulates a pedagogical vision of the world as nonunitary, multiplex, and fecund. This vision represents, to cite Lugones, a world "lived in the first person." Adopting Lugones' idea that individuals are "word-travellers" and that they inhabit "a multiplicity of voices, representations and experiences," Hernández emphasizes the power and promise of discourse in both the agonistic and playful strategies of self-constitution.

For Hernández, a feminist pedagogy of difference is one that validates subjectivity and agency. Agency is not characterized as a self-reproducing humanistic category or as a form of expressive self-referentiality, but rather assumes a dialectical character that speaks to the politics of both resistance and transformation. This resistance becomes part of the construction of a feminist counter-public sphere. In discussing the Mother's movement in Argentina, Hernández positions the role of critical agent within a discourse of critique and possibility, such that the social agent emerges as concrete actor, a political subject who situates herself within historical struggle. In doing so, she binds the practices of pedagogy, democracy, and discourse into metonymic relationships around a political imagery of emancipation. At the heart of Hernández's feminist pedagogy is the freedom to organize social encounters that will maximize the material needs and desires of the social subject.

Hernández places the concept of pedagogy within a radical democratic language so that teaching becomes interventionary—so that it can unsettle, displace, and rupture the constitution of knowledge, subjectivity, and social relations. Hernández's feminist pedagogy does not simply reinscribe or recover social difference at the level of classroom life, but rather offers as a condition of its possibility the instantiation of transformative praxis. Hernández is not content to subvert or relocate "the law of the Father" or unsettle the injunctive *pronunciamientos y declaraciónes* of the bourgeois academy. She is not content, in other words, to interpret the world, but advocates an epistemology of practice through which women and men are obliged to change the social, cultural, and discursive organizations that give rise to women's experiences and lives lived in servitude and subordination. Her feminist pedagogy in not merely descriptive or critically hermeneutical, but is fundamentally praxis-oriented.

Adriana Hernández offers a pedagogy of hope and social justice at a time when all of the "Americas" need it most. *Pedagogy, Democracy, and Feminism* is a welcome and important addition to the critical literature on schooling.

PREFACE

This book should have been finished in November of 1993. However, in November 1992, together with my husband Daniel and our daughter Mariangela, I started the journey of returning home to Argentina, after almost five years abroad. I say "started the journey" because it was much more than just a question of a long trip by plane.

In Argentina, I was overwhelmed by a diversity of demands such as housing, resuming my job, connecting with my mother and sisters, adjusting to having missed five years of the "lived history" of my country, and more.

My work on the book stopped for almost a year. I had neither a place to work nor the mental and emotional conditions necessary for the challenge. Finally, I was able to again consider my dissertation and address the issues I wanted to develop and extend in the book.

By the time I got back to my country, the neoconservative political trend was well established, as it was in Central countries (i.e. USA, England) and other countries of Latin America. In the case of Argentina, this meant the privatization of state companies and industries, and the re-organization through decentralization of the educational system in such a way that the state was no longer the main provider of the service. The social and political impact of these changes made me aware of how significant it was to renew discussions on democracy and the advent of counterpublic spheres as spaces of decision and action.

In this way, my work encompassed wider dimensions, constituting a particular challenge to my thesis which links pedagogy to democracy.

In the most fundamental terms, this book represents an attempt to remap the boundaries between pedagogy, feminism, democracy, and discourse. In rewriting this new space, I have been mainly concerned with the articulation of a politics of difference. Through such a journey of "crossing-borders," I hope to contribute to the work of teachers and cultural workers in general who engage themselves in the daily struggle of pedagogical practices.

INTRODUCTION

A PARTICULAR VOICE, IN A SPECIFIC TIME AND SPACE

... political theory must base itself on the initial premise that all persons, including the theorist, have a fleshy, material identity that will influence and pass judgment on all political claims.[1]

When I was working on my Doctoral dissertation, which finally became this book, I was thinking of the woman—myself—that came to the USA in May of 1988. At that time, I was carrying with me the tiredness of seven years of teaching within a sterile theorization locked in the discourse of methods. I was still full of the fear and the anger that a long period of political repression in Argentina had imposed on people as an everyday experience. At the same time, I hoped to find new spaces of reflection, a language to articulate my lived experience, and the means to re-articulate my theoretical baggage. By doing graduate studies at an American university I do not mean "visiting dream land" in an uncritical perspective. Rather, I intended to gain some material and emotional distance on my immediate context, to think not only from a different location, but from one that makes more explicit power relations—in the sense of being positioned as an outsider thinking with others.

Working as a full-time instructor in the School of Education at the University of Comahue (Argentina) in 1986, I became involved in a renewal project for the whole secondary level curriculum. This project was developed by the province of Río Negro within a politics of democratization of the educational system. I was assigned to the reformulation of the area of social studies, while also working within the restructuring of the general pedagogical practices of the classroom—with which all the teachers of secondary level were involved.

Working actively in this project, I became interested in the theorizing of the curriculum, a field of study that had been postponed for a long time in the country because of the political turmoil and repression of the last Dictatorship (1976–1983). Within the current process of democracy—starting in December 1983—the question of the curriculum emerged as a fundamental and urgent

1

aspect to be considered. Up to that point, the dominant tendency within the educational sphere was of a technological perspective. Although different curricular discourses overlapped in the formulation of a concrete project for schooling at the secondary level (and other projects inside the School of Education), there was still a problematic underlying logic involving the search for 'how to' recipes. Most of the discourses were organized along a psychological approach. For example, a developmental psychology centered on the adolescent as an essentialist category. Or a cognitive psychology (particularly Piaget and Gagne) centered around the learning process. Other discourses tried to open up a new framework by engaging socio-historical, political, and cultural aspects, a tendency that mainly stemmed from the tradition of critical pedagogy in Mexico.

Reflecting back on these issues, it seems clear to me that even in the more critical attempts to develop a curricular discourse by engaging the relations of school to the wider society, what was missing in these discursive articulations—either at the theoretical or common sense level of engagement—was a discourse of possibility that would really empower people for critical understanding and also set conditions for agency and change. In saying this, I do not mean that there was no awareness of oppressive institutional forms and practices, but rather that a multiplicity of circumstances conspired against concrete possibilities of transformation. Among these, for example, I can refer to the language and theoretical resources available at that time which were very much concentrated on critiquing phenomena of ideological and material reproduction in general, generating, in this way, a reductionist discourse of despair. Furthermore, at that time, the freedom of the newly democratic order manifested itself within the academic institution in the form of incredible amounts of diverse bibliographical material that had finally managed to cross the borders of repression and censure. Although this represented a very positive step, the disorganization of the distribution also meant that fundamental theoretical, historical, and political aspects of the material, much needed for its critical appropriation, were overlooked in a confusing dynamic of inclusion and exclusion. I still remember the joy and the domesticity of our way of sharing "new stuff" as hundreds of photocopies were passed around in a collective frenzy—since books and journals were either too expensive or not available. In this way, although these materials did contribute to the creation of a public sphere for discussion, they also too often became just fashionable discourses with a short life span and a disempowering effect. I recall reading school ethnographies—in the form of close accounts with no theorization—and not understanding their critical power. I can relate this event to Peter McLaren's experience of publishing his journal *Cries from the Corridor* without a theoretical framework and thinking it would speak for itself. He clearly states that "absolutely nothing is of unmediated availability to human consciousness. To 'know' anything is always an effect of power/knowledge relationships."[2] That mediating process, a critical and pedagogical one, was missing, indeed. I can also recall being stuck in theoretical constructs like Bourdieu's concept of "habitus," getting the general idea but not having the necessary framework to initiate a critical interpretation that would give me a sense of empowerment, positioning me—in Giroux's terms—as a "transformative intellectual."[3]

ABOUT PURPOSES

Contemporary forms of critical educational theory with their narrowed vision and truncated view of the possibilities opened by new theoretical perspectives have kept the field too insular. It needs to make new connections, take up new paradigms, and open up different spaces with new allies in order to work simultaneously on changing the schools and the wider social order.[4]

In an attempt to understand the complexity of the pedagogical problematic, I want to remap the linguistic, social, and theoretical boundaries among pedagogy, feminism, democracy and discourse. Although my analysis will be informed by my experience as a teacher in Argentina during the Dictatorship of 1976–1983 and the period of democratization that followed, the larger theoretical narrative of my work goes beyond those limits and engages wider cultural and political concerns. In re-writing a new space and creating new boundaries to reformulate the grounds on which educational and broader cultural and political questions are to be conceived and discussed, I want to take up these very elements and establish a new problematic. Such a problematic will specifically argue that pedagogy is central to any language of democracy. Equally important is the question that for any language of democracy to be taken seriously, it must link not only the pedagogical to the political but must be taken up in a way that engages the specificity of contexts in which people translate private concerns into public issues. For me, the theoretical discourse that offers the best opportunity for examining these issues is feminism: particularly a feminism that engages a politics of difference. That is, in expanding my analysis to discuss not only curriculum theory but wider pedagogical practices, I am extending the notion of the pedagogical so as to give it a political project. In doing so, I organize my work around a politics of difference informed by the project of critical democracy, making central the issue of critical pedagogy in its relationship to feminist theory. In this way, I am working with a politics of difference rooted in the project of democratic struggle, buttressed by traditions that come out of critical pedagogy and a critical feminism.

In chapter one, I map out the terrain of the pedagogical within the terms of a discourse of critique and possibility. In doing so, I address the question of defining pedagogical practices within broader paradigms that not only go beyond reproductive approaches, but place those practices within the field of cultural politics. This particular discursive construction links pedagogy to democracy as its necessary theoretical and ethical referent. That is, by moving pedagogy away from the dominant discourse of methods and 'how to' recipes, we enter a discourse that addresses wider social relations and power struggles. In particular, I address in this chapter pedagogical practices within a feminist theorizing that engages a politics of difference.

In the second chapter, as a further step in my work, I extend the language of critique and possibility by taking it up within the larger project of the discourse of democracy. In this way, I address democratic theory referring to it as a language, a particular communicative construction, and explore the specific radical possibilities it offers for the wider struggle of social change. In doing so, I am moving from the traditional liberal discourse of consensus to explore the emancipatory possibilities of a radical democratic discourse that takes into account a much needed politics of difference. Then, as an example of how this language of critique and possibility is linked to the notion of democracy and the pedagogical, I re-write the relationship between the public and the private sphere. In doing so, I establish a framework that supports discussion of the particular pedagogical value of public spheres in contesting existing structures of domination.

In the third chapter, I engage in an analysis of public spheres as spaces for democratic pedagogical practices within the particular emancipatory possibilities offered by feminist discourse. I explore the possibilities of the feminist counter-public sphere in a dual way: one, by placing myself within this space and engaging different theoretical conceptions of the private-public split in a process of argumentation and critique; and secondly, by looking at the Mothers' movement in Argentina as a concrete and particular example of a historically situated counter-public sphere and analyzing closely its practices—particularly in their pedagogical value—as overflowing traditional limits between the private and public.

In the fourth chapter, I show how the Mothers' movement still constitutes an active counterpublic sphere today. The Mothers have enlarged progressively their political commitments and continue to denounce and work against the multiplicity of situations of oppression. By transcribing portions of the dialogue I had with the Mothers, I intend to display their collective struggle during these past years and in the present, rather than to stress their individual testimonies.

In the fifth chapter, I extend my analysis of the interplay of pedagogy, feminism, democracy, and discourse to apply it to the rethinking of the pedagogical practices within the university setting. I concentrate on the problematic that emerges in the process of theory/discourse distribution and appropriation. The idea of pedagogy as a counterdiscourse and public sphere that articulates multiplicity of counterdiscourses is central in this discussion. In this chapter, I also develop both a set of criteria on critical pedagogy 'in action' and a reflexive recovery of concrete pedagogical practices that have already been enacted. The aim is to reflect on the operative dimension of critical pedagogy.

In the sixth chapter, I draw some conclusions that do not pretend to work as closure, but rather leave open the possibilities for further research and theorization.

In all six chapters, there is a shifting interplay of the terms pedagogy, democracy, and feminism around the idea of an emancipatory political project. In doing this, I engage dominant discourses, such as a liberal one on democracy, and I work with counterdiscourses—such as the discourse of radical democracy on the one hand or critical pedagogy on the other. I also consider how similar words take on different meanings relative to the positions from which they are used. This book frames these positions, as inscribed by the practices of class, gender, race, and other struggles, within a paradigm of emancipation. It fundamentally recognizes the formative effect of discourses both in their discursive and material dimensions, the pedagogical moments within them, and the necessity of democracy to provide a framework within power struggles in order to offer an emancipatory possibility against oppressive hegemonic social forms. In this way, while acknowledging material and structural forces, I try to develop a sense of agency by both engaging in readings that articulate a politics of difference and uncovering practices, like the Mothers' movement in Argentina, that overflow oppressive representations.

1

Remapping Pedagogical Boundaries:
Critical Pedagogy, Feminism,
and a Discourse of Possibility

The wider movements in feminist theory, poststructuralism, post-modernism, cultural studies, literary theory, and in the arts are now addressing the issue of pedagogy within a politics of cultural difference that offers new hope for a deteriorating field . . . Refusing to reduce the concept to the practice of knowledge and skills transmission the new work on pedagogy has been taken up as a form of political and cultural production deeply implicated in the construction of knowledge, subjectivities, and social relations.[1]

The refiguring of pedagogical practices within broader paradigms is a fundamental step in the extension of a democratic politics of transformation into spaces other than the school setting. We need to recognize, as educators and cultural workers in general, the changes in social theory that are taking place in different fields in order to respond to actual needs and develop more empowering forms of theory and practice.[2]

As already stated in the general introduction to this work, in taking into account the transformation that social theory has been undergoing, the purpose of this book is to remap the linguistic, social, and theoretical boundaries among pedagogy, feminism, democracy, and discourse. In doing so, I argue that pedagogy is central to any language of democracy. Furthermore, I argue that for any language of democracy to be taken seriously, it must link not only the pedagogical to the political but must be taken up in a way that engages the specificity of contexts in which people translate private concerns into public issues. Among the diversity of discourses available, feminism seems to me to offer the best opportunity for examining these issues, particularly a feminism that engages a politics of difference. That is, in discussing wider pedagogical practices, I extend the notion of the pedagogical so as to give it a political project. In doing so, I organize my work around a politics of difference informed by the project of critical democracy, making central as its primary constituent the issue of critical pedagogy in its relationship to feminist theory.

In this chapter, by arguing for a remapping of pedagogical boundaries, I will be sketching the movement of my thought in a way that illustrates the story of my theoretical journey or, better expressed, the broadening politicization of my consciousness and discursive baggage. Recognizing the link between the production of power and cultural production and, within the latter, pedagogical practices as producing knowledge, subjectivities and social relations is a journey in itself. This journey is both intellectual and political, since forms of knowledge production and subjectivity formation set the terms in which we perceive not only ourselves, but the physical and social world we live in.[3] In arguing for more emancipatory pedagogical practices, I propose more dialectical forms of learning and knowing that take into account the historicity and, therefore, the contingency of current structures of power and culture. That is, by engaging myself in this journey for change, I am trying to encourage others to join in the process and break with oppressive paradigms by taking up the ongoing struggle for more democratic forms of life.

I structured this chapter in three sections. In the first one, in a way that reflects the process I underwent, I try to come to grips with previous critical theoretical approaches, resignifying them both in terms of the discourse of critique they provide and the shortcomings they have in failing to develop more dialectical conceptualizations of structure and agency. Although this is not a thorough historical account, it seems important to me to point out some of the narratives that were more influential in Argentina after the democratic order was re-established, and to re-assess them within the framework of a discourse of critique and possibility. In the second section, after setting the main categories of critical pedagogy, I concentrate on the task of providing a more precise conceptualization of pedagogy, pointing at the remapping process it is undergoing by being recognized as a practice that takes place in multiplicity of spaces, besides the school setting, broadening its limits to cultural work. In the last section, having stated the unavoidable political character of pedagogical practices and the fundamental role of cultural workers in taking up questions of democratization and revitalization of public life, I proceed to explore the possibilities of a more radical democratic imaginary that engages a politics of difference. I not only engage myself in the kind of intellectual journey I think cultural workers should undertake, but I also try to broaden theoretical paradigms by addressing pedagogical practices within feminist theorizing.

IN SEARCH OF A PEDAGOGY OF CRITICAL CITIZENSHIP

Historically, traditional liberal educational discourses have discussed schooling as providing opportunities for individual improvement, social mobility, and economical and political betterment to marginalized sectors of the population such as the poor, ethnic minorities, and women. These discourses have been very much disseminated in Latin America through the different kinds of educational campaigns and programs funded by the United Nations and other international institutions—like the World Bank—within the diverse countries. The emergence of critical reproduction theory challenged this conception of education, rejecting the assumed neutral and apolitical structure of schools and pointing out that these institutions were social and cultural agencies very much involved in the legitimation and reproduction of dominant material and ideological conditions.[4] Stanley Aronowitz and Henry Giroux provide a critical discussion of the possibilities and shortcomings of three important theories within the reproduction paradigm of schooling which I consider important to address. These theories had a major impact in the first stages of theorization that the Argentine university engaged in at the beginning of the democratic order in 1984.[5]

The first model is the economic-reproductive, represented mainly by the works of Althusser, Baudelot and Establet, and Bowles and Gintis.[6] These theorists analyzed the links between the economic structure of society and the transmission of certain skills and knowledges to determined social sectors in order to perpetuate the current system. A fundamental concept here is the term "hidden curriculum" as it "refers to those classroom social relations that embody specific messages which legitimize the particular views of work, authority, social rules, and values that sustain capitalist logic and rationality, particularly as manifested in the workplace."[7] The strength of this approach includes a discussion of education and its interrelationship with the wider society, particularly the social restructuring of the capitalist economic system.

Another model is the cultural-reproductive, represented mainly by the work of Pierre Bourdieu.[8] The central tenet of this perspective is the analysis of the mediating role of culture in the reproduction of class societies, resulting in an empowering study of the dynamic of class, culture and domination. A concept fundamental in this perspective is the term 'habitus,' conceived as "a set of internalized competencies and structured needs, an internalized style of knowing and relating to the world that is grounded in the body itself."[9] This concept is significant in the sense that it moves the idea of learning beyond intellectual processes to acknowledge the body, senses and emotions in order to go beyond merely intellectual or rationalistic considerations.

The last model is the hegemonic-state reproductive one. Within this paradigm, the analysis is centered around the complexity of the role of the state in the educational system, leading to diverse discussions about credentialism, access, expertise and providing important categories to analyze content and form within the official distribution of knowledge. Gramci's conceptions of state and hegemony have been key categories in this work. Relevant and important work has been done by Michael Apple.[10]

It can be said that critical reproduction theory represented a challenging alternate discourse to traditional educational theory, but by not addressing questions of experience and agency it failed to provide a project of transformation that would enable educators to move from a feeling of despair to concrete strategies of change in light of an emancipatory vision.[11]

Another alternate discourse to dominant liberal educational theory representing a step beyond reproduction theory is resistance theory. This new approach considered the capacity of individuals and groups to contest hegemonic control, creating a new framework in which domination-resistance tension was apparent.[12] In Weiler's terms "the concept of resistance emphasizes that individuals are not simply acted upon by abstract 'structures' but negotiate, struggle, and create meaning of their own."[13] In this way, resistance theory provided the possibility to perceive human agency and action in the school setting: a challenge which reproduction theory had completely ignored. The work on resistance theory has been mainly undertaken by critical sociologists and cultural theorists associated with the Centre for Contemporary Cultural Studies at the University of Birmingham in England. A key work is Paul Willis's study of working-class boys, *Learning to Labour*.[14] Aronowitz and Giroux developed an important critical analysis of resistance theory which revealed its empowering elements and also its limitations.[15] According to them, a problematic aspect of resistance theory was the perpetuation of the division between structure and human agency, and the consequent failure to provide a dialectical perception of either. Additionally, resistance theory did not take oppression into account along lines of gender and race, and remained within the classical parameters of the economic structure. It also failed to point out how oppression and domination are internalized, creating the need for a critical psychology to uncover and transform those processes. It is important to mention Paulo Freire, the Brazilian pedagogue, who powerfully theorized this phenomenon of internalized oppression and developed a brilliant strategy through his conceptualization of conscientization and problem posing.[16] Resistance theory also limited itself to the analysis of overt acts of resistance by students, not considering other behaviors that are less visible and could be mistaken for acts of compliance.

Moving from reproduction phenomena to a definite focus on production phenomena more complex than resistance theory, critical pedagogy next constitutes the most significant and fertile source of critique and possibility in the current social and cultural theorization.[17] Critical pedagogy provides a dialectical perception of the relation between structure and human agency, recognizing the different processes of mediation through which teachers and students produce and reproduce their conditions of existence. Rather than getting stuck in a reproductive framework or romanticizing teachers' and students' acts of contestation in an unproblematic way, this approach perceives school settings as spaces where struggle and contradictions are enacted in no linear or determined way, giving place to negotiation and the development of a project of transformation. This project of transformation is what Henry Giroux calls a discourse of possibility. That is, to a needed but not sufficient discourse of critique we can add now a discourse of possibility that provides the elements to work for change.[18]

Critical educational theory makes available a whole set of empowering categories of inquiry, reconceptualizing pedagogy in ways that move away from both traditional conservative and liberal positions and also transcend reproductive paradigms of critique. But critical pedagogy is not a unified and coherent set of ideas, "it is more accurate to say that critical theorists are unified in their objectives: to empower the powerless and transform existing social inequalities and injustices."[19] Drawing heavily from Henry Giroux's work, the most productive theorist within this tradition, I would like to offer some of the key categories and conceptualizations that structure this new paradigm.[20]

First category: the expansion of the notion of the political as permeating the whole social order. Furthermore, power and control are understood not only in negative terms but also in their capacity to create a different social order.

Second category: the combination of a discourse of critique with one of possibility, empowering subjects to become agents in a process of both social transformation and also reaffirmation and reformulation of their histories and experiences in view of better and more emancipatory concerns.

Third category: the reconstitution of the teaching practice, moving it beyond either mere technical concerns or elitist professional interests, and conceiving of the teacher as a transformative intellectual in need of critically engaging current social and cultural forms within a wider project of transformation with other cultural workers.[21]

And the last category: the contestation of reductionist constructions of the school as a neutral space, recognizing it as a site of struggle among dominant and subordinate cultural practices along diverse axes of power such as race, gender, class, sexual orientation.

Finally, the question arises: how is it possible to define pedagogical practices within this critical framework in a more concrete and precise way? What terms are necessary to conceptualize the relationship between culture and pedagogy?

WHAT IS PEDAGOGY, ANYWAY?

Pedagogy refers to a deliberate attempt to influence how and what knowledge and identities are produced among particular sets of social relations . . . a practice through which people are incited to acquire a particular "moral character."[22]

What I find empowering in this definition is that it addresses questions of both knowledge and identity production and their connection within power relations. How knowledge gets produced/communicated and how students participate in the process as either objects or subjects are fundamental political aspects to be taken into account. All these elements speak for a practice that is about much more than teaching strategies or concerns of mere practitioners. That is, pedagogy refers to a necessary dynamic of theory and practice with political and ethical concerns leading the process of reflection and reorganization. These concerns should be structured around a fundamental emancipatory discourse of equality, freedom and justice, and should aim at a democratic vision.

Within the academic tradition of the Argentine university, which is mostly European, questions of pedagogy according to the dominant paradigm—which ignores radical discourses such as the Freirean, accusing it of trespassing disciplinary borders—refer exclusively to the philosophy of education, while teaching and instruction constitute the field of didactics. Within a different tradition, pedagogy is not a common word for those in the American university educational field who do not have contact with critical theory, since this perspective is the one that reclaims and reformulates the term. Rather, the language of technique articulates talk about "learning," "teaching" and "educational objectives." Although differently located, what is missing from both dominant approaches is an understanding of how pedagogical practices are about much more than removed philosophical foundations or the immediacy of teaching strategies. Pedagogical practices, in a broader sense, are about the kind of social visions they would support.[23] That is, all those involved in pedagogical practices cannot avoid the fact that these take place in concrete settings within the wider society in which questions of power are articulated among such issues as What is to be included and what excluded as legitimate knowledge for learning? Or, whose story is worthy most? What kinds of social relations are being promoted? What forms of learning are articulated that, at the same time, configure ways of engaging and perceiving ourselves as subjects or passive objects within the world we live in? What kind of representations are being constructed "of ourselves, others, and our physical and social environment."[24] This mode of inquiry situates us within a completely different tradition as we reinterpret pedagogy as a form of cultural politics. This discursive organization, by acknowledging power as productive, allows one to see how it works through people, knowledge and desire in a normative way, which means, in turn, organizing life and its possibilities in a certain form and direction.[25] There is a tight link between power and culture that determines certain modes of semiotic production which are "historically and economically constituted by the social forms within which we live our lives."[26] Therefore, "the production of various forms of image, text, gesture and talk . . . have to be understood as integral to the possibility of either the reproduction or transformation of any social order."[27] Where is the work of educators located within this conceptualization? Obviously, within semiotic production. Furthermore, the term educator should be expanded beyond the limits of the school setting and, best of all, the term of cultural worker might be an alternate frame for this more liberatory perception. After all, pedagogical practices, as put forth in this book, take place within diversity of institutional contexts and not only within the school setting. That is, spheres of cultural production in general are engaged in the construction and negotiation of knowledge and identities. Therefore, pedagogical practices speak to broader cultural and social concerns. Pedagogy, as already stated, is about cultural politics. If that is so, pedagogical practices require the involvement not only of educators, but of cultural workers in general to engage in the task of reforming all spheres of cultural production according to a democratic vision "as part of a wider revitalization of public life."[28] In the words of Henry Giroux, "It is imperative for cultural workers to provide in their work and actions the basis for a language of solidarity and a project of possibility as part of a new vision and attempt to rethink the meaning of democratic citizenship . . ."[29]

ABOUT RADICAL IMAGINARIES AND TRANSFORMATIVE PEDAGOGIES

Pedagogy is simultaneously about the knowledge and practices that teachers, cultural workers, and students might engage in together and the cultural politics such practices support. It is in this sense that to propose a pedagogy is at the same time to construct a political vision.[30]

As stated earlier, it is important that educational theory take into account theoretical developments in a diversity of fields within social theory. The failure to do so would produce impoverished levels of reflection and shortsighted political projects with no empowering effect relative to the current challenges facing education in general and democratic forms of life worldwide. Diversity of forms of domination and oppression, like sexism, homophobia, racism, unquestionable views of cultural heritage, and growing bureaucratic control within schools, are calling for a renewed democratic imaginary.[31] By this, I mean a project of life, and a vision of a better social and material world. This new vision should be a radical democratic one speaking to difference, forms of dissent rather than enforced consent, change, and multiple forms of power and authority. A critical pedagogy that produces diversity of knowledge and subjectivities contesting domination and oppression is a fundamental practice for more egalitarian forms of life. This notion of radical democratic forms of life is expanded in the second chapter of this book.

In the context of the current feminist movement, especially with regard to feminist work oriented toward uncovering the link of specific oppressions of women to the larger structure of capitalism, and to oppressions of other groups—gays, minorities, the working classes, and so on—issues such as difference, the possibility of engaging in dialogue in spite of heterogeneity, and women's representations through language emerge in the process of theory making. That is, feminist pedagogy linked to critical and liberatory concerns that extend to other oppressed groups besides women, seems to offer an empowering articulation of those questions that are also part of the work of postcolonialism, poststructuralism, critical literary theory, and other theoretical fields that are undergoing radical renewal.[32] This section concentrates on the particular work of Maria Lugones and Elizabeth Spelman.[33] Analyzing a concrete articulation of theory and experience not only speaks louder and stronger, but also provides living voices and experiences to this process of reflection. Therefore, written in the tradition of critical pedagogy, feminist pedagogy, and a critical cultural perspective, I argue for a more radical democratic imaginary by considering important aspects developed by Lugones and Spelman such as the ideas of plurality, difference, love and voice. I also try to incorporate these ideas into a pedagogical proposal. Several general assumptions underlying this analysis are:

- The need to develop a theory by theorizing the practice, what Giroux would refer to as a theory emerging in concrete settings, although not collapsing in them, in order to analyze them critically and get into action "on the basis of an informed praxis;"[34]
- The need to use a language of critique and, at the same time, a language of possibility to not only recognize injustice, but also to develop a project of emancipation;
- The use of concepts, such as voice and dialogue, not only in the tradition of critical pedagogy, but also enriched with the perspective of Bakhtin's theory, to deconstruct and reconstruct the terrain of everyday life;[35]
- The need to have a conception of the subject, in the context of the current controversy about this topic, to develop political action and a sense of agency.[36]

Before analyzing the elements of Lugones' and Spelman's work that I find empowering, I will provide a general overview of the content of the articles selected. The two articles I chose are organized in a two step process: a dialectic beginning theorizing lived experience and going back to practice with a transformative proposal. In "Have we got a theory for you!:Feminist theory, cultural imperialism and the demand for the 'woman's voice'" (1983), they state the necessary conditions and considerations required for women of different races and cultures to engage together in feminist theorizing, dealing with the concepts of difference, plurality, solidarity, dialogue, voice, identity, experience, talking, and hearing. They articulate all these concepts in a way reminiscent of Gayatri Spivak:

> The problem of human discourse is generally seen as articulating itself in the play of three shifting "concepts": language, world, and consciousness. We know no world that is not organized as a language, we operate with no other consciousness but one structured as language-languages that we cannot possess, for we are operated by those languages as well. The category of language, then, embraces the categories of world and consciousness even as it is determined by them.[37]

This statement points at both the role of the material and the discursive in shaping life, but it stresses the effect of language in an attempt to focus theoretical discussion around the need to transform language as part of the wider strategy to change the world. Work on discourse and language constitutes an important trend in contemporary social theory. Lugones and Spelman take up the issue of language to assert the necessity and the possibility of creating new concepts, and of developing a theory to name the "others," in this case women's experiences.[38] In this process of women naming, theorizing and interpreting their own experiences, the hierarchy between theorists and doers is erased. There is no place for an elite giving a language to name; rather, this place should be taken by all women—and all those in positions of oppression—to make sense of their own lives. With respect to this, I can recall Gayatri Spivak again when she asserts the importance of recognizing a subaltern subject-effect to transcend the danger of working with intellectual traditions so entangled with the sociocultural context that diverse forms of domination like imperialism, patriarchy, racism, slip elusively into the mind.[39] Additionally, when Lugones and Spelman ask the following, they posit the need of the outsider and the insider to engage in a dialogue where they are both outsider and insider with respect to each other.

> To what extent are our experiences and their articulation affected by our being a colonized people [outsider], and thus by your [insider] culture, theories and conceptions?[40]

The motivation for engaging in dialogue is love and friendship as opposed to domination and oppression.[41] An ethical concern, indeed.

In the second article, "Playfulness, 'world'-travelling, and loving perception" (1987) written only by Lugones, she describes the experience of what she refers to as "outsiders" to the mainstream, and characterizes a practice that is recognized as the only way of theorizing. This way, world-travelling with a playful attitude, meaning a loving way of being and living, is to Maria Lugones the condition for enriching feminism with plurality, a central need of feminist ontology and epistemology within the context of the current competition in feminism. Although the articles deal with many aspects and considerations, this text addresses only those that are crucial in the constitution of a democratic imaginary and the development of a transformative feminist pedagogy.

The first consideration is the question of dialogue. Lugones states that in order to engage in dialogue, it is necessary not to erase differences; rather, these should be preserved as a precondition for dialogue. In the prologue (written in Spanish), Lugones argues that solidarity should not be confused with absence of difference, because solidarity requires the recognition, understanding, respect and love which leads women to cry in a different way. Furthermore, dialogue requires two voices, not one, because one would mean somebody's oppression and silence.

The question of difference, structured along a power tension, is both a postmodern and a postcolonial concern. Lugones's theoretical position once again recalls Spivak, specifically with regard to what she refers to as speaking in first person and third person. Spivak would refer to the first person as "the privatist cry of heroic liberal women," and Lugones and Spelman as "white-Anglo, middle class, heterosexual Christian or not self-identified non-Christian women."[42] But why do they refer to the first person as being white women? Because they are the ones in the place of privilege doing theory, while the third person has been the place of blacks, Hispanics, working class, and other women. On the other hand, although Lugones and Spelman recognize the categories of insider/first person, outsider/third person, they consider them a duality—rather than a binary—opposition, not excluding one another, both interplaying and interchanging. Lugones and Spelman argue, "we write together, . . . when we speak in unison . . . there are two voices and not just one."[43]

As a second consideration, the place Lugones and Spelman assign to women's experiences and their articulation in language seems important to me. That is, the question of what is said about experience, who says it, and to whom. Talking about women's experiences is of particular importance because what is being said and what ideas are held about them, have material consequences. Lugones and Spelman assert, "our experiences are deeply influenced by what is said about them."[44]

There is the need to hear the "woman's voice"—although not in an essentialist conception, rather as located within historical and cultural terms—as a central concept to the development of feminist theory. Here Lugones and Spelman introduce a particular conception of the subject, one they refer to in these terms,

> The concept of the woman's voice . . . presupposes a theory according to which our identities as human beings are actually compound identities, a kind of fusion or confusion of our otherwise separate identities as women or men, as black or brown or white.[45]

The subject for Lugones and Spelman seems to be somewhere in the middle between the humanistic one, as pre-given, and the decentered one, as a structural determination. Their concept of the subject seems to me the one Mikhail Bakhtin refers to as a multiplicity of voices.[46] Voice recalls the idea of utterance and, consequently, must be placed in dialogue. Language, as dialogue, consists of social phenomena always in the process of becoming. Individuals do not receive a ready-made language at all, they enter into social communication and in this process their consciousness is constructed, being active in the transformation of the communication process. This aspect is of special importance since it imparts a sense of agency; it stresses the role of the individual in the transformation process as well as the role of the community. In this way, multiplicity is not only recognized in the different voices that emerge in the community, but also in what Vygotsky refers to as inner-thought, an internalized dialogue.[47] Finally, this subject of multiple voices seems to be what Lugones and Spelman refer to as "compound identities," as the different voices depending on the positions the subject has taken or has been given; that is to say, a positioned subject.[48]

As a third consideration, I would like to take into account the way Lugones and Spelman reflect over the theory-making process, to which they refer in the significant subtitle of the article as "Ways of talking or being talked . . ."[49] One aspect is that a theory can be useful if it helps to make sense of one's life through the use of concepts that are not foreign. Furthermore, a theory would be useful if it helps one understand her/his location in the world using new concepts that do not mystify the world, but rather, empower one to realize if one "is responsible or not for being in that location."[50] The most powerful claim the authors make while uncovering power relations is when they state that a theory, to be useful, should not only reflect the "situation and values of the theorist," but also those of the "people it is meant to be about."[51] In an insightful inquiring style through which they posit fundamental pedagogical questions, the authors ask:

> As we make theory and offer it up to others, what do we assume is the connection between theory and consciousness? Do we expect others to read theory, . . . believe it . . . and have their consciousness and lives thereby transformed? Do we think people come to consciousness by reading? Only by reading?[52]

With these questions, Lugones and Spelman challenge oppressive pedagogies that conceive knowledge as something ready to be transferred, and learners as passive objects. As an alternate emancipatory position they pro-pose the active participation of learners as subjects in the process of knowl-edge production, since knowledge itself is a dynamic. Undoubtedly, there is the ethical need to listen to the voice of "the other" in the process of theory-making, and also to extend this process beyond academic intellectuals to other groups in order to enlarge public spaces, empowering them to reflect and theorize over their everyday life, and to practice making connections with the wider society. As an explanation, Lugones and Spelman add that "theory-makers and their methods and concepts constitute a community of people and of shared meanings."[53] There is an explicit connection here between the sociocultural and the theoretical-epistemological, a connection also stressed by Spivak in the relation of "the micro-politics of the academy" to the "macro-narrative of imperialism."[54] By asserting the idea of commu-nity, the authors challenge Basil Bernstein's position of insisting that "the-oretical terms and statements have meanings not tied to a local relationship and to a local social structure."[55] Rather, Lugones and Spelman believe a the-ory is made in a specific time and place and is closely related or enacted by particular interests.

Lugones's idea of "world"-travelling is the fourth and last consideration. She succeeds in explaining how individuals are dependent on each other to be understood, intelligible, integrated; to make sense. Being dependent does not mean being subordinate, a slave or a servant; rather, being dependent means travelling to another's worlds in order "to be" through loving each other. Lugones would say that by travelling to another's worlds allows us to "under-stand what is to be them and what is to be ourselves in their eyes," a necessary condition for plurality, which is also a central feature of feminist ontology and epistemology.[56] Lugones's idea of "world"-travelling may be compared to Henry Giroux's proposal of a border pedagogy, a practice that enables people to recognize the partialities of all discourses, experiences, and codes, and which stresses the need to become a border-crosser in order to decenter ourselves and remap meanings, concrete relations, and lives in more equalitarian ways.[57]

At this point, I would like to articulate the ideas of plurality, difference, love and voice in the development of a transformative feminist pedagogy of dif-ference by posing the following questions:

- In what sense is dialogue through difference significant for pedagog-ical practices, and particularly for the wider practice of social change?
- In what way is the conception of the subject as "compound identities" significant? What about agency?
- Considering pedagogical spheres as places where knowledge and the-ory are produced, in what sense is Lugones and Spelman's proposal of a community-building theory empowering?

- In what ways does Lugones' proposal of "world"-travelling offer both a language of critique and a language of possibility?
- What is the political project arising from this pedagogy of difference?

The common sense approach to difference in education has been to act as if there are no differences, as if "we are all equal." This approach attempts to erase diversity and to unify people in a consensual discourse. But to treat people "as if" there were no differences does not make it so. When we realize whose educational discourse is adopted in the name of equality, we come to understand that difference is merely negated for the benefit of those who are not defined, or are less vulnerable with respect to categories such as sex, ethnicity, or class: that is to say, the white male middle class. This discourse creates concrete oppressive situations where many are silenced: for example, blacks, who are forced to become "raceless" if they want to succeed in the current educational settings; or women, who are forced to acquire male rational patterns to be accepted in the academy; or even minority women, who are forced to accept definitions of women as women in feminist theorizing, being silenced with respect to their race, class, religion, sexual alliance, and ethnicity.[58] The invisibility of the white middle-class pattern, and, in turn, the invisibility of white middle-class heterosexual Christian women or, as Lugones would say, "not self-identified as non-Christian," becomes dangerous in the process of silencing. A transformative feminist pedagogy should be one that addresses difference in all its possibilities within power relations in a constant process of contestation against concrete oppressive practices. In the words of Henry Giroux,

> The notion of difference must be seen in relational terms that link it to a broader politics that deepens the possibility for reconstructing democracy and schools as democratic public spheres.[59]

Dialogue, as Lugones posits, enables women and other oppressed groups to interrelate among themselves, to talk together in different voices, addressing the differences that make them outsiders and insiders with respect to each other.

Addressing the second question, the conception of the subject as "compound identities" points to a pedagogy that recognizes not only multiplicity of subject positions, but also the tension among them. Minority women, in particular, can begin to conceptualize themselves in terms of what it means for them to be women as blacks, lesbians, poor, Hispanics, or Jews. Furthermore, another aspect that Lugones and Spelman mention, and I would like to stress, refers to women having to define themselves as women outside their communities. This results when Anglo-individualistic patterns are disguised as universal. For example, this is the case of Hispanic women resisting patriarchy by alienating themselves from their communities. What may be a powerful strategy for white women turns to be a painful alienation for Hispanic ones. I see as very problematic a feminism that fails to address transformation in the context of communities, limiting agency, and reducing definitions of self to individualism. I use the term community recognizing difference within it, not ignoring diversity under an impossible and oppressive homogeneity. Maria Lugones, arguing for the need to travel through others' worlds in a playful and loving way as opposed to an imperialistic one, states:

> We are fully dependent on each other for the possibility of being understood and without this understanding we are not solid, visible, integrated; we are lacking.[60]

Any pedagogical practice is about the production of subjectivities. A transformative feminist pedagogy should disclose how subjectivities—particularly gendered—are being constructed and/or represented outside and inside the school setting, and enhance the development of "compound identities." A pedagogy of difference not only has to assert students' multiplicity of voices, but also deconstruct them, see how they have become what they are, challenge problematic sexist and racist assumptions within them, and reconstruct them.

Pedagogical practices not only construct subjectivities, but also produce knowledge, theory. The issue is how to articulate different partialities, different discourses, different voices, in the process of theory-making. Lugones and Spelman argue for a non-imperialistic theorizing process, one that rejects universal claims and reductionism. I would add, a theorizing process that takes place in other spaces besides the Academy and recognizes partialities and confronts their limits without excluding those being theorized. A pedagogy of difference generates knowledge in community to serve all those involved in it, as opposite to a production of knowledge by an elite to serve its own interests. Lugones and Spelman point out,

> It is one thing for both me and you to observe you and come up with our different accounts of what you are doing; it is quite another for me to observe myself and others much like me culturally and in other ways and develop an account of myself and then use that account to give an account of you.[61]

The idea of a community building theory and producing knowledge disarticulates the hierarchy between theorists and doers and extends the process of inquiry, interpretation and contestation to those historically marginalized and excluded at different levels: Third World countries, women, blacks, students, gays, and others.

With respect to the particular production of knowledge in the classroom as a process of articulation and interpretation of the students' experiences, one of the main objectives of a feminist pedagogy of difference will be to make explicit the assumptions of the sociocultural context that provide a particular meaning to the multiplicity of the utterances in the dialogue. Reading and writing should be seen as productive activities through which meaning emerges and can be analyzed in the final texts the students produce. The general assumption underlying the previous statement is that the social uses of writing, the values implied, and the forms it takes all vary across historical time and cultural space. Therefore, reading and writing take on an ideological dimension that cannot be abstracted because through them students not only learn skills but have access to particularly defined cultural knowledge and social relationships.[62]

In relation to the questions about Lugones's concept of "world" travelling, I would like to stress her concept of world as "a construction of life," either dominant or nondominant, as a constructions of relations of production, gender, and race. These worlds—a rejection of a unified one—are necessarily inhabited by people, either real or imaginary, dead or alive. This is a powerful concept in that it enables disclosure of how life may be represented in a multiplicity of ways which make sense to concrete people or not, in ways they understand or not, in ways they accept or not. Even more, Lugones says that by describing her sense of a "world," she means "to be offering a description of experience, something that is true to experience even if it is ontologically problematic."[63] This is really a woman asserting women's experiences in a powerful and meaningful theorizing process, much more than a mere celebration of experience.

From a pedagogical perspective, this concept of world as lived in the first person seems to me very important because it makes more visible the living multiplicity of voices, of representations, of experiences, that make people "world"-travellers. Traveling as a relational shift from having one subject-position to having a different one according to the world or worlds inhabited at the time, not only helps us to get to know and understand others but should be applied to do so. Even more, traveling is something that minority people do more of because of their marginalization, although it has to be done also by those in positions of domination albeit in a loving and playful way. Lugones opposes a conception of play as uncertainty, opened to surprise and self-construction, to an agonistic conception of play as competitive, conquering, and imperialistic. A pedagogy of difference encompasses from the outset ideas of "world"-travelling, love, and playfulness, as a means for recognizing and disentangling all those worlds women and other marginalized groups inhabit. This is a fundamental way to come to know how different they are in each world, to get to know others in their worlds, to reconstruct themselves and others in an emancipatory way, having in mind a visionary communal world of equity, solidarity, caring, freedom, and justice.

A pedagogy of difference requires that both men and women recognize that emancipation is not just freedom from power over us, but much more, freedom of our power over others. This suggests an ongoing and interactive process of contestation to concrete situations that legitimizes the expression of different voices differently.[64]

Finally, the political project coming from this pedagogy of difference is one of democracy; but a conception of democracy that, in the light of the current limitations and reductionism to which the term has been subjected by conservative discourses, needs to be revised and reconstructed. It seems to me that a concept of radical democracy takes into account the richness and multiplicity of strands that are at play in a pedagogy of difference allowing them to come together in a common struggle. It is, then, toward radical democracy that a feminist pedagogy of difference might lead us.

The following chapter considers the task of analyzing current democracy theory, concentrating particularly on the discussion of fundamental categories necessary for the development of a more radical conceptualization in terms of the possibilities it offers for more egalitarian forms of life.

2

Informing Pedagogical Practices:
Democracy and the Language of the Public

... neoconservatism ... is incapable of realizing the 'libertarian' values it affirms—above all, those of freedom of choice, mutual aid and self-reliance. Male dominated households, a capitalist-directed economy and the strong state, which are the trump cards in the hand of neo-con-servatism, directly contradict its professed anti-bureaucratic principles. This suggests that only the democratic tradition, and not neo-conservatism, can genuinely defend the libertarian ideals of mutual aid, demo-cratic accountability and the taming and restriction of state power.[1]

By setting the terms of the discussion, neoconservatism is attempting, I would add very successfully, to appropriate 'history' by both providing a language to signify the complexity of the current moment, and also by subverting concepts and meanings that have historically been the core of the libertarian tradition.

The current severe economic restructuring taking place in western Europe, with particular dramatic characteristics in Latin America, makes us face the fact that this is a structural crisis that not only affects economic relations but too the complexity of political, social, and cultural relations.[2]

Is this crisis being recognized? Or is it being perceived as a temporary phe-nomenon? What are the terms within which these 'changes' are conceptualized?

My purpose in this brief introduction is not to get into an analysis of what neo-conservatism is, or what are its detriments to the welfare state, but rather to make a reference to the economic and political context that gives meaning to the discussions about what a democratic discourse may offer to expand its current possibilities.

In the particular case of Argentina's process of adjustment to the 'new world order,' different changes are taking place, such as the privatization of fun-damental state companies/industries, greater flexibility in the labor market, and the restructuring of the educational system which downgrades the role of the state as a provider of services to civil society. The discourse accompanying these processes is the focus here. In a recent document published by the National Ministry of Culture and Education which addressed a specific audi-ence of parents, teachers and students, they state:

Education for an age of change. If there is something that character-izes the world we live in, in the proximity of the third Millennium, this is change. . . . Technologies change, pushed by the scientific-techno-logical revolution. Ways of facing health issues and illness change. Systems of production and commercialization change. Maps change, new nations appear and others disappear. Employment and knowl-edge required for work and for social life change. . . . It is necessary for the education of Argentinians to change too. And this needs to be as fast as possible, for the country—its people, its children and its youth—to be in conditions to better adapt to this incredible process of transformation. The dramatic truth is that if we do not adapt, we will be left on the margin.[3]

The language used makes no reference to relationships with the wider social order, nor to any historical context. Even more, change just seems to be a natural process that has to do more with continuity and evolution than with power tensions articulated around diversity of social, political and cultural issues.

Again, I want to point out the need to articulate a language that would enable us to reconceptualize current problematics in order to perceive them in their full complexity and understand their implications.

PEDAGOGY AND DEMOCRACY

As stated in the previous chapter, pedagogy, conceived as a practice that pro-duces particular knowledge and subjectivities, is an unavoidable political issue in the sense that it refers to forms of cultural production. That is, pedagogy is about much more than schooling and the classroom. Pedagogical practices take place in a diversity of spaces in the wider society, and they are about large concerns such as which forms of life and which worldviews are the ones to be legitimized.[4] In this chapter, after situating pedagogical practice within the boundaries of political discourse, I want to analyze the language of democ-racy as the one offering the best vision for personal and collective development in terms of values such as freedom, equality, and solidarity.

This chapter is divided into distinct but related sections, each of which addresses different categories essential for the construction of a more emanci-patory and radical conception of democracy. The reader should keep in per-spective that the wider goal of this chapter is to generate a space of critique around the issue of democracy. That is, she/he should avoid getting caught in a sterile analysis of the categories in themselves; they often serve only as dis-cussion openings as a means of unravelling fundamental questions of power.

In the beginning, the importance of language/discourse as a fundamental meaning-making practice is referred in the constitution of identities and in the process of self and social transformation. From there, the question of discourse as the key element constructing social action is discussed, particularly the language of democracy as that which holds the most radical possibilities for change. Within this language of democracy, two central terms of political life, power and its relation to politics, are analyzed.

In order to make explicit the necessity to take up a politics of difference in the construction of a more emancipatory democratic order, I draw heavily on the works of Herbert Bowles and Samuel Gintis, Ernesto Laclau and Chantal Mouffe. In doing so, I engage liberal discourse both in its possibilities and shortcomings relative to the construction of a radical democracy and the development of pedagogical practices that account for the formation of knowledge, the self, and collective identities. From there, I discuss the private-public split that, although considered also a liberal legacy, needs to be moved beyond these limits in terms of the importance of its implications for democracy. The discourse of the private and the public, in being integral to the dominant language of democracy, suggests that this debate about the public and private sphere is inextricably a debate about democracy and pedagogy.

All the elements mentioned above constitute a fundamental ground on which to understand the constitution of the category of public sphere as a discursive platform for which resistance, participation, collective deliberation and decisionmaking take place as both a moment of critique and an alternative to existing conditions.

MAKING SENSE: LANGUAGE AND EXPERIENCE

> . . . to alter the terms of public discourse one must change the experiences people have, and to restructure experiences one must change the language available for making sense of those experiences.[5]

The need for a language to articulate our experience and give it meaning—although partial and always open to further resignification—is a fundamental aspect in every process of self and social transformation.[6] The language that is available to us provides a frame of reference with which we understand, reflect, name and also constitute our actions, feelings and desires, both as individual and collective beings. As many theorists have already stated—among others Ferguson, hooks, Anzaldúa—we use the language that is available to us, which most of the time is only the dominant language.[7] By dominant language I mean not a unified one that controls all aspects of social life, but rather certain patterns that are hegemonic within different sectors and areas of social life. For example, there is a dominant language within the Academy known as the Master's discourse, which does not take into account women's experiences and ways of knowing. This language pretends to stand for a neutral and universal subject which, in fact, is white, male, and middle class.[8] At the same time, this does not mean that there are not alternative languages and discourses within the Academy that resist this dominant pattern. Although I understand dominant discourse as a multiplicity of signifying and institutional forms, I believe that they are connected, mutually influencing each other and creating, at times, an overdetermining discourse. For example, both the discourse of patriarchy and the discourse of capitalism when intertwined permeate the whole social structure—influencing sites as different as the family, the market, the state, the educational system, and the church.

The way we relate to language varies according to our diverse subject positions—i.e., female, Asian, middle-class, gay. This means that some times we are being empowered by it and others disempowered. Or rather, discursive power works in a way that renders some people powerless, devoid of any control over their lives. In conclusion, usually people on the margins do not have an alternate mode of expression to articulate their experiences or to resist the patterns that are oppressive to them.

Given these conditions, it is of primary importance we recognize the power of discourse to constitute people's subjectivities. Therefore, it is a fundamental task of pedagogy to engage meaning-making practices. In doing so, it is possible to create the conditions that address discourse as a dynamic terrain of struggle subject to an ongoing process of redefinition through which the lives of people can be transformed and liberated. In this regard, this chapter deals mostly with a theoretical language that in one sense is detached from my immediate personal experience, but at the same time, does not mean I cannot connect to it. By dealing with political theory, I appropriate and transform this theoretical language, making it speak to me, and as a result my own understanding and actions get reorganized in ways that I experience as liberating. The power tension involved in this process opens to me the possibility to perceive and construct myself as a political subject.

Next we move from consideration of discourse as constitutive of the self, to its possibility as a bonding instrument for collective action.

DISCOURSE AND THE CREATION OF SOCIAL ACTION

> . . . if common social position precedes social action, solidarity and common interest (both its existence and its content) come into being only through concrete communicative and organizational practices.[9]

The introduction of the linguistic model into the general field of social sciences provides the framework for rethinking issues such as personal rights or citizenship, for example, as part of a discourse as opposed to conceiving them as either liberal or reactionary. That is to say, those terms as part of a contemporary dominant language, although carrying a history with a particular conceptualization, can be used at the same time by very different and oppositional social sectors for their own specific interests. Referring to the notion of citizenship, Hall and Held state

> ... it seems to be the case that citizenship belongs exclusively to neither Right nor Left, nor indeed to the centre-ground. Like all the key contested political concepts of our time, it can be appropriated within very different political discourses and articulated to very different political positions—as its recuperation by the New Right clearly shows.[10]

Arguing further this point, Bowles and Gintis reject the expressive Marxian conception of political discourse as part of the superstructure. For example, within the limiting borders of the expressive theory of action the discourse of rights 'remains but a reflection of an essentially bourgeois and elitist political philosophy.'[11] This conceptualization does not allow us to understand why the discourse of rights is being held by so many different and opposing social movements and continues to be a source of resistance and liberation. Furthermore, Bowles and Gintis strongly reference the fact that the essentialist position of considering terms and conceptions as belonging or reflecting a certain exclusive position undermines the possibility of explaining or understanding why people as individuals get together and engage in action conducive to social change.[12] This constitutes for me a key point for apprehending the contingency of issues such as political action, collective identities, solidarity, and bonding, and for redefining them in non-essentialist terms; terms that allow for capturing these phenomena in their relational complexity and multiplicity.

How do individuals make sense of shared experiences? How do they organize in temporary and contingent movements towards social transformation? Bowles and Gintis argue that discourse is 'a set of tools' and as such provides the elements to organize and structure collective action.

> People use tools to forge the unities that provide the basis for their collective social practices ... Lacking an intrinsic connection to a set of ideas, words, like tools, may be borrowed.[13]

Although I agree with this statement, I would point out that words, and language in general, have the appearance of such an intrinsic connection. That is to say, words recall a whole set of ideas. But language as dialogue among concrete people consists of social phenomena always in the process of becoming. Individuals do not receive a ready-made language at all; they enter into social communication and in this process their consciousness is constructed, being active in the communication process. Richard Quantz and Terence O'Connor express this idea clearly when they argue, "This dynamic conceptualization of the individual's relation to the social world . . . presumes that every individual has an active role in affecting the communication process and, hence, in continuing the ongoing reshaping of the culture."[14] This aspect is of special importance because it suggests a sense of agency; it stresses the role of the individual in the transformation-emancipation process as well as the role of the community.

Another aspect to take into account is that discourses refer to much more than words. They include "such aspects of communication as flags, uniforms, and architectural form." In sum, discourse has the ability to bond people and organize action, creating the conditions for achieving personal and collective projects.[15] This approach provides the elements for theorizing both the formation and action of individuals as social actors and the process of transformation of social structures through their activity. It seems to me that this conceptualization is the basis for an empowering theory of action: individuals both get constituted and constitute themselves through discourse and this, at the same time, works as a bonding element for action. Furthermore, individuals can participate in this process of constituting themselves and through it they can come together to build a dynamic unity for social change and transformation. The aim of this chapter is to reflect on the language of democracy as the bonding and constitutive element for social action and transformation. Also, it aims to critically analyze some of the most central terms and topics of political life in order to open the possibility of transforming experience while creating a more liberating public discourse. Issues such as power, action, change, citizenship, and community knit the web of meanings in political culture, providing a necessary articulation of everyday life experiences and setting the terms either for participation and continuous transformation or for disempowerment and stagnation.

Before discussing the language of democracy in itself, I will make explicit in what terms I understand questions of power and politics, two fundamental aspects of political discourse.

RETHINKING POLITICS AND POWER

Reconsidering contemporary political and economic philosophy, Samuel Bowles and Herbert Gintis point out how the radical democratic tradition not only provided the elements used to conceive the integration of politics and economics, but also the elements used to conceptualize themes such as oppression and politics in a more comprehensive and distinctive way; a way that seems to enrich the possibilities for rethinking and actualizing democratic theory and practice.[16]

With respect to power, Foucault sets the terms that allow political theory to depart from the traditional unified conception to show how power works in many ways and in a diversity of spaces. He states,

> The omnipresence of power . . . , it is produced . . . in every relation from one point to another. Power is everywhere . . . because it comes from everywhere.[17]

Perceiving power not as unified or as if deployed from only one source creates the conditions for detecting its workings in different forms and within different spaces. Said theorizes power around representation as productive and inhibiting, being wielded by intellectuals associated with the dominant social group.[18] Gramsci distinguishes power as both negative and repressive, and also as positive and educative.[19] Williams refers to it as permissive and constitutive and, at the same time, as exerting pressure and imposing limits.[20] Finally, Foucault points to the ability of power not only to censor, block or exclude, but also to produce desire, knowledge and truth.[21]

In what ways are these conceptions of power important for re-thinking collective action, democracy? It seems to me that by recognizing power in a diversity of forms and as produced by multiple sources, allows for the identification of its working not only at the local level but also within concrete strategies. The demystification of power as an all encompassing and unified structure that cannot be resisted, subverted, or dismantled has an empowering effect.

According to Foucault, relations of power are not in a position of exteriority with respect to other types of relationships—either cultural, economic, or else.[22] It seems important to me to analyze more closely this interiority of power with respect to different social relations, because it provides an interesting infrastructure for re-thinking pedagogical processes within a multiplicity of cultural spaces, an issue I will take up later. To discuss this question I am going to draw heavily on Bowles and Gintis's conceptualization of power and action.

Bowles and Gintis state, "power is exercised through social action."[23] Paraphrasing: action is understood by these theorists in terms of a practice, either individual or collective, and it has as its aim the transformation of a certain object of social life. Their categorization of action is worth quoting at length.

> When the object . . . is part of the natural world, we speak of the practice as appropriative . . . When, however, the object of the practice

includes the rules of the game themselves—that is, the stabilization or transformation of a structure of social relations—we speak of the action as political . . . We will . . . consider a practice as distributive to the extent that its object includes the distribution and redistribution of positions and prerogatives within a given set of rules of the game. Finally, when the object of a practice includes the transformation or consolidation of the tools of social discourse, we will term the action cultural.[24]

These categorizations of practice do not exclude one another; an action can be political and cultural at the same time. Although certain social sites are identified for a particular action performed within/by them—i.e., the state with politics—diverse actions are present within each site. I will expand on this topic.

As Foucault pointed out, the conceptualization of power as heterogeneous and not only negative, but particularly productive, exercised through a multiplicity of social actions, contributes to the reconstruction of the conception of politics as "not simply about the manner in which power adjudicates competing claims for resources."[25] The dynamics of power and politics produce knowledge, people, and ways of life. Therefore, this dynamic is about much more than issues of distribution, about more than getting, but rather, as Bowles and Gintis say, about becoming.[26] This is the pedagogical aspect of politics that is not always taken into account. I will consider this issue again in the section about pedagogical practices.

The field of politics is a shaping wherein conflicting interests and values are always at work. Conflict and struggle are constitutive of the political process and through it new interests and values are produced in an ongoing and never final movement. When conflict and struggle are articulated by discourse in the form of collective oppositions, there is a possibility for change and transformation. It is discourse, the bonding element within this multiplicity and complexity of the social, that constructs the solidarity and the common interests necessary for this change to occur.

What is the strength of the discourse of democracy? What is the framework offered by democratic language for re-thinking power, collective action, and pedagogical practices?

ABOUT DEMOCRACY

As I stated before, it is the articulation of experience within a certain language that allows for its understanding and transformation. Historically, it was the language of democracy that "provide[d] the discursive conditions which made it possible to propose the different forms of inequality as illegitimate and anti-natural . . . to make them equivalent as forms of oppression."[27] Democracy, through the times, has been and still is the discourse that sets the terms for critique of current affairs and institutional orders and creates the basis for their change. Although, we should agree, the language of democracy is anything but uniform. Democracy carries the most diverse and conflicting meanings and concepts which are not always liberating enough, and sometimes not liberating at all. What kind of democracy am I going to stand for? Certainly, a radical one. One that stands for equality, social justice and solidarity, enhancing at the same time popular sovereignty and individual liberty.

Chantal Mouffe and Ernesto Laclau provide a fundamental approach to the analysis of what democracy ought to imply to be truly liberating by arguing that the democratic discourse of equality and liberty should be extended to diverse areas of social life in an ongoing process.[28] Through the introduction of the idea of radicalizing equality and liberty, the question of a liberal democratic framework is unavoidable. Liberalism, through its concept of pluralism, adds a fundamental critique and transformation to the traditional idea of democracy as consensual, as being able to represent an all encompassing conception of what a good life is. Mouffe points out that we must accept the inevitability of conflict and antagonism as fundamental and constitutive elements of political life. Therefore, instead of perceiving those traits as problematic, as an obstacle to a moment of total stability and homogeneity, they should be perceived as the healthy traits that allow for a constant transformation and prevent that moment of stability as a menace to the liberties of the members of society that do not coincide with what the "general will" at a certain historical moment might be. According to Mouffe and Laclau, modern democracy should be pluralistic, having as its objective "the creation of a chain of equivalence among the democratic demands found in a variety of movements—women, blacks, workers, gays and lesbians, or environmentalists—around a radical democratic interpretation of the political principles of the liberal democratic regime."[29] In this way, liberal democracy seems to me to be able to offer fundamental elements for a discourse of radical and pluralistic democracy that articulates at the same time equality and difference, the individual and the social, the political and the ethical, all in an open process of negotiation.

Bowles and Gintis develop an analysis of democracy that also seems to provide an important perspective. They conceive democracy as having two fundamental tenets: popular sovereignty and liberty. These elements take into account both the social and the individual aspects of life and allow at the same time a conceptualization of the tension between social determination and choice. According to the authors, liberty refers to the individual freedom of action within diversity of social spaces. Therefore, "liberty entails freedom of thought and association, freedom of political, cultural, and religious expression, and the right to control one's body and express one's preferred spiritual, aesthetic, and sexual style of life."[30] With respect to popular sovereignty, they mean that "power is accountable . . . to those affected by its exercise."[31] Since power, as we have already seen, is displayed in a multiplicity of social sites, not only in/by the state, there is another whole new dimension that implies the opening to democratic control of areas previously closed to it. The consequences of this opening are particularly significant within the conception of liberal democracy that considers spheres such as the economy as private, and therefore, not accountable. Bowles and Gintis reformulate the idea of popular sovereignty in terms of plurality. Building on the idea of power as heterogeneous and being deployed in different spaces of social life, they reject the idea of a unified popular will or consensus—like Mouffe and Laclau. Popular sovereignty, consequently, is also heterogeneous, plural. The conception of democracy, once more, is radicalized as a necessary aspect for contemporary democratic life.

THE PEDAGOGICAL CHALLENGE:
HOW PEOPLE GET TO WANT WHAT THEY WANT TO BE?

I understand the idea of pedagogy within the terms of a critical pedagogy that addresses fundamental questions about the production of knowledge, the production of subjectivities, ways of knowing, and learning. My main purpose in selecting the expression 'pedagogical challenge' for the title of this section is to draw attention to the productive aspect of diverse social practices. That is to say, the dynamics of power at the interior of diverse cultural spaces and practices set the conditions and limits within which personal and collective capacities are developed, thus producing certain ways of knowing, understanding, acting, communicating, and bonding.[32] In recognizing this phenomenon, I want to point out the possibility for transformation offered by pedagogical practices in the sense that they constitute deliberate attempts to interrogate particular knowledges and subjectivities, as well as influence the process of their production.

Up to now, this book reflected on the possibilities that the language of democracy offers for transforming experience and developing a public discourse wherein justice, participation, difference, freedom, equality, and solidarity set the ethical conditions. In this process, I pointed out the elements of liberal discourse that were important for a conception of a radical plural democracy. Next, I concentrate on the analysis of those aspects of liberalism that have to do with the constitution of subjects and collective identities. Furthermore, I will concentrate on those elements that, in setting the conditions for the production of certain knowledge and subjectivities, constitute a fundamental field to be engaged by critical pedagogical practices.

Once more, I want to make clear that the focus of this work is the articulation of a substantial discussion about the emancipatory possibilities of pedagogical practices. Therefore, the particular theoretical articulations and terms of political theory selected in this chapter on the subject of democracy such as public/private or chooser/learner, are largely a pretext for unravelling more fundamental questions about power and politics.

To draw from liberal political theory to rethink the question of democracy is a quite controversial direction. Liberalism posits many problems in terms of its procedural conception of democratic institutions and the idea of the individual as ahistorical. But, as Chantal Mouffe argues, there are many discourses within what is considered the philosophy of liberalism, and this, by no means, is a unified doctrine.[33] Therefore, while some aspects of liberalism enrich democratic thinking, others might impoverish or contradict it. In the previous section, I made clear the importance of the principle of pluralism for democracy. In this section, I will analyze the obstacles that the liberal discourse of individualism presents for grasping the process of constitution of the subject and collective identities.

As I stated in the section on power and politics, change occurs when conflict is articulated within a discourse that creates alliances among subjects and opens the possibility for collective action. This particular theorization differs from others that do not recognize the subject as social—for example, liberal individualism—or, if they do, they might not perceive the aspect of choice as necessary and integral to the process of social transformation, as in classical Marxism. My purpose is to explore this issue within a framework that makes visible the question of human development, of learning, which is to say, the pedagogical function that democratic discourse and institutional practices might play in the constitution of individual and collective identities.

As a starting point, I will begin with an analysis of liberalism as a discourse that creates spaces and partitions through which social life is represented. It is worth referring to part of Bowles and Gintis' quotation of Michael Walzer's view in this respect.

> . . . liberal theorists preached and practiced the art of separation. They drew lines, marked off different realms, and created the sociopolitical map with which we are still familiar . . . Liberalism is a world of walls, and each one creates a new liberty.[34]

Within the liberal framework, society is no longer represented as a totality, but rather as structured in compartments which, although keeping certain relations among themselves, are independent and separate units governed by different logics. The ease with which social spaces are divided and understood as completely separate seems to me to be one of the biggest obstacles of liberalism as a means for understanding political and social life. Particularly when it comes to the question of the private-public split wherein the issue is not so much about different institutional spheres as it is one of relational distinctions.[35]

Related to this question of dividing society into spaces, Bowles and Gintis develop an analysis of social theory that seems to me of fundamental importance for understanding the possibility of pedagogical practices in different areas of social life. The authors refer to the phenomenon of 'isomorphism of sites and practices' as a problematic suffered by contemporary social theory.

> In this view, a particular practice is uniquely associated with a particular site of which it is ostensibly characteristic; the economy with appropriation and distribution, the state with politics, and family, church, and media with culture.[36]

Within this framework, it is not possible to perceive how the structure of the economy, for example, has also political and cultural functions besides those which are appropriative and distributive. The economy does not only refer to labor (appropriative) or to the distribution of positions within the factory, it also refers to both the establishment of certain social relations (political) and the characteristics of social discourse (cultural).[37] That is to say, the different sites of social practice are not identified with only one activity, although social appearance might make it appear so. Political, distributive, appropriative, and cultural practices are all present at once in diverse sites. These practices, in terms of the productive effect they have constituting ways of seeing the world, especially our knowledges and subjectivities, represent the terrain for the engagement of pedagogical practices in a process of critique and change. Or, rephrasing Foucault's conception of power to apply it to pedagogy, I would say that pedagogy is at the interior of political, cultural, distributive, and appropriative practices in the sense of representing a strategy for the interrogation and transformation of knowledge, interests, desires, and subjectivities in a complex dialectical process. This helps us understand how a certain economic or political order has productive effects in the sense of creating, for example, a certain way of understanding the world according to somebody's interests or story. In this way, particular settings and practices should be engaged according to their specificity by a diversity of pedagogical practices; practices that Henry Giroux would refer to as pedagogies of place.

Returning to the issue of the division of society into diverse spaces: the partition that offers a key position for unravelling further the pedagogical question is the one that liberalism creates by classifying individuals in a binary opposition, one that Bowles and Gintis refer to as choosers and learners.[38] These categories represent a certain logic that produces people in a certain way, a way that hides domination. Choosers, as rational agents, are supposed to be the holders of liberty, a liberty that they exercise either in the public or the private realm. Learners, on the other hand, do not have liberties or participation in politics, and democratic norms—in the sense of liberty and equality—are not applied to them. Historically, the question of who gets to be a chooser or a learner has varied through struggles of power organized along the categories of gender, race, and class. That is to say, for example, that women, blacks, and people that did not own property were not considered choosers at all.

The categories of chooser and learner are closely linked to two other categories, voice and exit, which Bowles and Gintis take from Albert Hirschman and use to critique the liberal conception of a theory of action. Bowles and Gintis explain exit and voice, respectively, as

> . . . exercising one's freedom to choose independently of collective sentiments, and entering into mutual, reciprocal, and participatory action with others to achieve commonly defined goals.[39]

Individuals are conceived as asocial, as being able to choose in a totally autonomous way. Interests, the motivation for action, are considered as pregiven by liberalism. Therefore, the activity of individuals as agents is perceived in terms of exit. Bowles and Gintis's analysis is worth quoting at length:

> Individuals exercise their rights through market and ballot box. Both present a "menu" of alternatives . . . The power of the chooser is limited to his or her ability to abandon a product or a political party—that is, to "exit." The market economy and the liberal democratic state, then, stress exit to the virtual exclusion of voice, and representation to the virtual exclusion of participation.[40]

If interests are pregiven and the individual as chooser is already completely formed, there is no language to articulate the productive effect that the market, for example, or other social spaces have in constituting and shaping interests, needs, and desires (i.e., people). Within these terms, the conception of citizen is one limited to the isolated action of an individual that chooses (a client). People get together around preexisting objectives/interests (according the interest groups conception) and there is no possibility for articulating the formative, bonding, and constitutive effect that this political process has. Therefore, the oppressive or democratic shaping possibilities of institutions and practices remain hidden. There is no language to acknowledge this phenomenon or develop an empowering theory of action in collective terms, beyond just those that are individualistic. This problematic points to the need for developing pedagogical practices that uncover the productivity of cultural phenomena and call into question oppressive institutions and practices working for their transformation. A central component of this project is the notion of democratic public sphere as an ideal space for liberatory pedagogical practices. In the following section, I discuss the politics at work in the question of the private-public split. I offer fundamental distinctions that seem to me to overcome binary oppositions and, in doing so, provide the ground upon which to analyze the concrete topic of the public sphere that is discussed in chapter three.

THE PRIVATE-PUBLIC SPLIT

The Liberal Legacy

Although the partition of the social space into the realms of the private and the public is originally part of liberal political theory, we can argue—as I did in the beginning of this chapter—that these terms are part of a discourse, and this by no means reflects or translates a preexisting state of affairs. Furthermore, this discourse can be appropriated and used by very different political positions. Therefore, redefining public and private spheres is a fundamental aspect of democracy rather than "just a liberal concern," since it encompasses the fundamental issues of access, participation, equality, consensus, and difference.

Liberalism understands the public space to be the state, and the private space to be the family and the capitalist economy.[41] It seems to me that this conceptualization has become part of what I would call common sense, a generalized and non-critical way of conceiving what is public and private, as if these categories were reflective of reality. If we add to this aspect the question of 'isomorphism of sites and practices,' we find that the state is perceived—within this common sense—not only as the unique public space, but also the unique site of politics, while the economy and the family are considered both private and apolitical. In analyzing the whole construction of the public-private split, I intend to concentrate on the question of politics, on how the shifting boundaries between both terms vary according to the different interests and forces at play. The main purpose of this reflective process is to move from the problem of the private-public split as an ideological construction that oppresses, to a politics of distinctions that protects the right to keep private that which people do not want others to know but, at the same time, does not oblige things to be a priori out of public discussion.[42]

In defining the private, liberalism "limit[s] the admissible range of application of its basic terms relating to freedom, equality, and democracy" by conceiving this space as apolitical.[43] In this way, the workings of power within this sphere get disguised and domination remains hidden. Although Marxism does not offer an alternate definition of the private and the public and considers them a purely liberal invention, it does successfully show that spaces considered private, such as the patriarchal family and the capitalist economy, are the site of domination.[44] If both the private and the public are clearly a matter of political distinctions rather than institutional spheres, politics is not the criterion to differentiate them, but rather a tension between both that should be taken into account.

In accounting for the liberal conception of the private and public, it is essential to thoroughly historicize the issue in order not to be caught within the universalist and abstract pretensions of liberalism, missing the patriarchal roots of the phenomenon. In her feminist critique of the public-private dichotomy, Pateman cites Eisenstein's assessment on this dangerous tendency. He states that "the ideology of public and private life invariably presents the division between public and private life, . . . as reflecting the development of the bourgeois liberal state not the patriarchal ordering of the bourgeois state."[45] The liberal division of civil society from the private sphere of the family is a division between men's reason and women's bodies.[46] Reason is conceived as transcendental and disembodied, or rather with a male body in opposition to the desires and feelings embodied in women's bodies. Through this ideological construction, women are at odds within the public sphere because they represent everything that the public is not. Consequently, when women find their way into public life, they get positioned in a very different way and must struggle with contradictions and misrepresentations when exerting the role of citizens, a role that has been primarily defined in terms of the use of force and the bearing of arms. The original division of private-public in terms of family/women and civil society/men, then gets transposed within civil society—men's world—in the form of the state/public and economy/private.[47] How is it possible to get out of this construction of two separate spheres and move political theory away from this historical encasement towards more liberating conceptualizations?

The Personal is Political . . . But Not That Much?

One of the cornerstones of feminism is the recognition of the private/personal as political. This means that aspects of everyday life—such as child care, language, parenting practices—should be open for discussion and criticism since all of them can be spaces for either oppressive or liberatory practices. Liberal feminist Jean Bethke Elshtain resists this conceptualization because she fears that defining the private as political will open it to the intervention of the state.[48] In this way she falls into the traditional liberal conflation of state and politics. David Held, although recognizing the need of a broader notion of politics that addresses all systems of power, also seems to fall into the same trap when he states:

> By making politics potentially co-extensive with all realms of social, cultural and economic life, it opens these domains to public regulation and control.[49]

What does he mean by public? The state? If so, it is a very narrow and unified conception of it, one that does not allow us to conceptualize mediating spaces of collective participation in between the individual and the state. Thinking about a diversity of arenas for decisionmaking and community action presents a completely different perception of the public; that is to say, a heterogeneous public. On Held's view, would a narrower conception of politics make spaces like the family or the school much more free? Held seems to get caught in the liberal fear of the despotic state, a fear that does not address other sources of domination and oppression. He also states:

> While a broad concept of politics is defensible and necessary to the adequate consideration of the problems and questions of democracy, it must be thought through carefully in relation to a conception of the limits of the justifiable reach of democracy.[50]

Held does not explain what he means by 'justifiable reach of democracy,' but there seems to be some problematic assumption of democracy and the public (centralized in the state) as holding most of all control and negative power. Or, perhaps, he does not worry particularly about control itself but about who exerts it. Although I certainly agree with his concern for the protection of privacy in the context of its current invasion by bureaucracies, it seems to me that he is still caught in defining the private as that which the public excludes, rather than what people want or have the right to keep from public scrutiny. There is a different tension in this conceptualization, one that moves the weight of control from a formal regulation of what is public and private to the people's right to decide what is so. Furthermore, if the democratic order that Held has in mind is one constituted just by a representative democracy, one that currently works without delegates being effectively accountable and recallable, I can understand, and even agree, with Held's concern about the "reach of democracy."[51] Furthermore, the public space as it currently works in democratic orders that are almost exclusively representative—political parties, legislative institutions, etc.—is highly bureaucratized, not reflecting at all the constituency's opinion but rather its own interests as a sector in itself.[52] Undoubtedly, there is a need to decentralize the conception and practice of what is public, and to open the possibility for rethinking power as more horizontal and playing within the multiplicity of spaces wherein decisionmaking and public debate are possible. The contribution of social movements has been fundamental to this issue.

With respect to the private, instead of using the expression private space, Held refers to 'a sphere of the intimate' as the one in which—unlike the public—the actions of people do not have "systematically harmful consequences for those around them."[53] Although he uses a wider conception of politics, he seems sometimes to fall back into the traditional collapse of public/political. For example, Held states

Clear criteria will have to be found for demarcating the public and the political from the sphere of the intimate, and for defining the limits to legitimate legislation in the latter realm.[54]

Both the private and the public are political, both embody the workings of power in diverse and intertwining ways. A final criteria will never be found. Perhaps the real question is about maintaining a process of ongoing critical analysis to see which interests get served and which disregarded in the multiple workings of power.

Towards Alternative Constructs

There are other approaches to the private-public split which offer more liberating alternatives and distinctions which are worth considering. The main purposes in reconsidering and reconstructing this dichotomy would be the need to: first, go beyond binary oppositions in order to recognize links and overlapping interests and concerns such as how one sphere is constructed upon the other; and second, to keep a realm of the personal, of that we do not want to share with others, and of that which, at the same time, would not be determined a priori to be private.

Bowles and Gintis make a substantial analysis of private and public spaces providing what seems to me to be an emancipatory criteria for the division: the norms of liberty and democracy. Within these terms, a public sphere would be one in which both norms apply, while a private sphere would be one in which only the norm of liberty applies. Furthermore, they state that

> . . . a sphere of social life is to be considered public if its operation involves the socially consequential exercise of power . . . By an "exercise of power" we mean an action that causes others to act in ways they otherwise would not . . . By a socially consequential action we mean one that both substantively affects the lives of others and the character of which reflects the will and interests of the actor.[55]

I refer to the criteria offered by Bowles and Gintis as emancipatory because they address the question of power and, consequently, open the consideration to issues of domination. Unlike liberalism, this is a discourse that articulates oppression in concrete settings such as the patriarchal family and the capitalist economy. The application of democratic norms is not relegated anymore to just a formal sphere of rights in the realm of the state, rather democratic norms get grounded in the material everyday-life conditions of the people.

On what grounds is there a need to maintain the spheres of the public and the private? Bowles and Gintis state:

The liberal defense of freedom requires a sphere of social life that is both private and moral.[56]

But Iris Young points out,

The purpose of protecting privacy is to preserve liberties of individual action, opportunity, and participation. The claim of any institution or collective to privacy, to the right to exclude others, can be justified only on grounds of enabling a justified range of individual privacy.[57]

The way I see it and the point of departure from which to answer this question is the concept of a pluralistic democracy. As I have already stated in my analysis of democratic politics, the liberal concept of pluralism is fundamental for modern democracy in that it expands the range of application of personal rights to address the issue of difference and to show the impossibility, also the danger, of a fully consensual social order. In this way, the radicalization of equality and liberty creates the need to maintain a space as private; a relational space, rather than institutional, as defined in terms of individual rights in an ongoing process of deliberation.

While I stress the need for keeping a space as private, I also stress the need for a public realm as one in which particularly popular sovereignty is at stake. The radicalization of democracy implies the expansion of accountability into sites where the 'socially consequential exercise of power' is at play and where, currently, people do not have much of a say—in schools, for example.

How and where do we draw the line? After all this analysis it becomes obvious that private and public spheres are not completely different and separate spaces. As Iris Young states, "private and public do not easily correspond to institutional spheres, such as work versus family, or state versus economy."[58] The map of the private-public is one with overlapping borders; borders determined in an ongoing process of discussion around issues and aspects of concrete persons and everyday life. A discussion that should be held publicly through discursive contestation because it is a democratic concern, indeed.

CONCLUSION

In this chapter, I have argued that the language of democracy is essential to the practice of pedagogy. By re-reading democratic theory and drawing from the writings of contemporary theorists that critique late capitalist society, I have provided pedagogy with a political project. This project turns away from traditional concepts of democracy. A pedagogy that is conceived as a concrete practice oriented to enhance personal and social possibilities has as a necessary condition the interrogation of all social forms and forms of power within democratic terms. Understanding democracy as both a language of critique and possibility allows me to articulate human development in terms of the concrete situatedness of the social conditions that enable or restrain, empower or disempower, its process. Therefore, addressing issues of power and domination and talking about the politics of certain pedagogical practices is unavoidable.

I would like to stress, once more, that my purpose has been to open spaces of discussion by engaging diverse theoretical approaches around the issue of democracy, which I closely relate with a particular conceptualization of pedagogical practices. Therefore, many categories and terms analyzed have worked as a pretext to prepare the terrain for critical consideration of the notion of democracy and public sphere and, why not, to exercise the enactment of the latter.

Having thus far set the framework of democracy for pedagogical practices in general, the next chapter considers, as a particular pedagogical practice, the fundamental role of feminist public spheres for transforming the gendered self and for contesting existing structures of domination. Feminist public spheres are spaces of liberatory pedagogical practices in the sense that they offer women—but not exclusively women—the opportunity to come to consciousness in community and articulate their opposition, both in theoretical and pragmatic ways, to oppressive social forms.

3

Inhabiting a Split:
Feminism, Counterpublic Spheres,
and the Problematic of the Private-Public

> The logic of the feminist counter-public sphere must thus be under-
> stood as ultimately rational, in a Habermasian sense, that is, not in
> terms of any appeal to a substantive idea of a transcendental disem-
> bodied reason, but in the procedural sense of engendering processes of
> discursive argumentation and critique which seek to contest the basis
> of existing norms and values by raising alternative validity claims.[1]

The purpose of this chapter is the exercising of the process of argumentation
that Felski refers to in an attempt to enact the possibilities of feminism as an
oppositional and transformative discursive arena around the issue of the private-
public split. I explore the possibilities of the feminist counter-public sphere,
which I consider fundamentally pedagogical, in a dual way: first, by placing
myself within this space and engaging different theoretical conceptions of the
private-public split in a process of argumentation and critique; second, by looking at the Mothers' movement in Argentina as a concrete and particular example of a historically situated counter-public sphere, analyzing closely its practices—particularly in their pedagogical value—as overflowing traditional limits
between the private and public. Sometimes both dynamics interrelate; at other
times, I specifically engage in the process of theoretical argumentation without
grounding it in the concrete experience of the Mothers.

In the beginning, I provide some elements to contextualize the line of my
thought and position myself—an Argentine woman—in terms of the issues and
questions I raise. I also give an account of the circumstances in which the Mothers' movement emerged in Argentina setting the first elements for a further
process of critique. Following this introductory moment, I develop two distinct
theoretical sections. In the first, I confront the problematic reconstruction of
the private and public by Jean Bethke Elshtain, trying to show the shortcomings
of the liberal framework that keeps her tied to oppressive constructions of

women.[2] In the second section, I offer an alternative reading of the private-public split moving it to a wider framework of discussion: the consideration of the subject of feminism, the tension between Woman-women. The logic I follow consists of interrogating the traditional constructions of private and public spheres in terms of who is/are the subject/s supposed to inhabit those spaces.[3] The tentative answer, which is open to further problematization, would be that Woman, as an abstract construct, is confined to the private; but women, as concrete historical beings, cross borders into the public—although in restrained conditions—subverting any attempt to establish fixed boundaries. Finally, I devote a section to the consideration of the empowering possibilities of a conception of (feminist) counter-public spheres or, in other words, a feminist reading of the public sphere that takes into account a politics of difference. For this purpose, I draw on the writings of Nancy Fraser and Iris Young, going beyond the limitations of the Habermasian reading of the bourgeois public sphere.

THE CONTEXT OF MY THOUGHT

At the start of 1990, in the context of a course on the politics of sexuality, I engaged myself in the painful and challenging task of reflecting on women's issues and feminist issues in Argentina. In this work, I concentrated specifically on women's political positions and practices in the concrete historical process of democratization. Some of the issues I addressed were:

- Within the last fifteen years of political turmoil, in what terms have women's subjectivities been produced or positioned in Argentina?
- How did women react to these subjectivities and, at the same time, how did they position themselves?
- In what ways did women contribute to the process of democratization, to a transformation of the concept of politics and, specifically to a politics of gender?

ARGENTINA: WOMEN FLOODING A
NORMATIVE MATRIX OF INTELLIGIBILITY

Within the context of the extreme repression of the 1976/1983 Dictatorship—during which the popular sectors were the most oppressed, there was a substantial reduction of social and educational services, and neo-liberal economic policy destroyed the internal market—women were addressed as mothers. The normative discourse of the Military regime was expressed in terms of nationalism (nazi-onalism?)—a militarist political culture which stressed the values of machismo, female subordination, heroism, and patriotism. The normative sexuality was heterosexism, and the imposed performativity was negatively displayed in terms of punishing homosexuality, long hair for males (beards and mustaches), pants for women, and unmarried men and women living together. Butler, it seems to me, would refer to this phenomenon as:

> The appearance of an abiding substance or gendered self, . . . a gender core, is thus produced by the regulation of attributes along culturally established lines of coherence.[4]

This normative sexuality that still lurks today in the common sense of many people, cannot tolerate ". . . the dissonant play of attributes that fail to conform to the sequential or causal models of intelligibility," these being either feelings, attitudes, or hair styles, thoughts, even dreams and body language that escape and flood, and at last subvert the so called given.[5]

During this period where everyone had an assigned role, women were one of the main targets of the normative discourse of the Military regime, particularly in their role as mothers. Feijoo states that mothers were considered, "[the] privileged guarantors of . . . a long term period of social restructuring."[6] This restructuring is the so-called Process of National Reorganization where the armed forces represented the fathers, women the mothers, and young people the sons and daughters.[7] But, I would ask, what kind of mothers? The guardians of the order of life, the moral ones? The way one group of women answered to this way of constructing their subjectivities (as moral, passive, altruistic, vicarious, restrained to the home) was by constructing an alternative political model based on sacrifice—overflowing the traditional self-sacrifice—rather than by rational negotiation.[8] Women, through the organization of Madres de Plaza de Mayo—referred to from now on as the Mothers—challenged the Military and not only reclaimed the lives of their children, but they denounced the systematic use of state repression and terrorism as a means of government.[9] By doing this, the Mothers overflowed the traditional model of femininity as passive objects of history. The Mothers, defending what traditionally they have been in charge of: life, flooded the traditional borders ". . . of the private sphere of the household and [entered] the autonomous space of public and political expression."[10] Feijoo shows how the Mothers, without the explicit purpose of changing patriarchal ideology or abandoning the normative femininity, ". . . produced a transformation of the traditional feminine conscience and its political role."[11] The new model of femininity, the subverting of the naturalism and morals of motherhood, seems to me to have gone into the public sphere and made life and love political. Which is to say, they made the personal political.

The division of the terms private and public, present in most of the studies—even in my own discourse—became a pivotal point for me from which to reconsider the politics of gender, feminism, and democracy. Furthermore, I began to problematize the binary opposition private/personal-public/political, which seemed to me a dead end and a limiting situation for feminist thought. As an example of the problem perceived, a current study on women's politics in different countries of Latin America—*The Women's Movement in Latin America*, edited by Jane Jaquette (1989)—limits the analysis of women's "success" to their political participation using traditionally male patterns.[12] In this work, success is measured either in terms of the number of women deputies, or women's "crisis driven" political participation, or, on the contrary, women's total depoliticization.

A PROBLEMATIC RECONSTRUCTION
OF THE PUBLIC AND PRIVATE

Another example of a limited analysis of the private and public is the book *Public Man, Private Woman: Women in Social and Political Thought* written by Jean Bethke Elshtain. Her purpose in the final chapter, after analyzing different historical approaches to the public and private, is to offer an alternate position—which she claims steps outside any attempt to provide a totalizing answer—by using a theory and a politics of limits.[13] In the development of her arguments, Elshtain starts by stressing the need to locate the female subject within concrete and local conditions,

> . . . moving away from the abstracted, disembodied 'products' of social forces . . . This female subject, . . . must be approached as an active agent of a life-world of intense personalization and immediacy.[14]

Although I certainly agree with these statements, I do not understand Elshtain's following move, which is to totalize feminism as a threat to this "personalization" by making a reductionist interpretive reading of certain texts; for example, de Beauvoir's *The Second Sex*, or works such as those of Daly and Firestone.[15] She asks

> . . . does any feminist political thinker really want to . . . relocate female subjects and reconstruct the matrix of their traditional identities by substituting the terms of universal, bureaucratic socio-economic imperatives that, as women achieve a public identity, they lose this other world and the values embedded with it entirely?[16]

She seems to be caught in the binary way of thinking the private as essentially female and the public as male: that is to say, two substantially different institutional orders with no connection between them. Furthermore, in terms of her statement, there seems to be only one public, as if it's a given—an essentialist and totalizing conception that does not go beyond the "bourgeois" public sphere.[17] This is a curious appreciation especially when women's actions have been historically enacted as alternative and contestatory public spheres, showing the importance of the public as multiple to further democracy. According to Elshtain, for women to become public individuals involves an either-or way of thinking, since her feminism, being liberal, is reduced to a struggle that just gives women access to the men's world without the aim of transforming the internal logic of the order.

Her final claim seems to me to be "let's keep the private the way it is." Certainly, the private she is referring to is the realm of the family, which she considers to be a universal, pan-cultural, and transhistorical institution. At this point, Elshtain has left far behind her claim of a politics of limits and locality. Getting into a totalizing discourse, she builds on questions and statements that look for universal answers, truths, and origins. For example, she tries to legitimize the existence of family beginning with the question: "What is the nature of man?," which serves as a first step for portraying the familial institution as the humanizing and socializing agency par excellence.[18] She strongly attacks any form of institutional child care, which she collapses with what seems to be the "classic" liberal fear of a totalitarian state—either on the extreme right or on the extreme left—and she ends up stating:

> The feminist political thinker must similarly ask at what price she would gain the world for herself or other women, utterly rejecting those victories that come at the cost of the bodies and spirits of human infants . . . the feminist concerned with a reconstructive ideal of the private sphere must begin by affirming the essential needs of children . . . Only then should she move to a second level of exploration and challenge by pursuing the creation of her idea on this moral foundation.[19]

At this moment, I see Elshtain holding to the old and oppressive cliches that nourish women's guilt by reminding them that they owe themselves to others, that they should remain self-sacrificing.

- What is the feminism Elshtain challenges?
- What is the feminism for which Elshtain stands?

It seems to me that she holds the very essentialist position of the feminine as biological, nurturing, and restricted to the private sphere of the family, which exists very much independent from the public and is defined as either the realm of the state or the logic of the market. Elshtain has been caught in the dominant patriarchal and liberal politics of representation of the private and the public, taking for real, natural, what is just a social construction—a partial and historical one—that has served to oppress women in multiple ways. Curiously, she stated that she would spend less time in the reconstruction of the public because,

> . . . it stands in less need of a defense and reaffirmation within feminist political discourse than our besieged sphere of the private.[20]

Certainly, it is an amazing reading of current every day life wherein women are struggling through their actions to be recognized in public spaces, and in political action as legitimate agents of change and transformation transcending the local. But Elshtain's analysis of the public completely lacks a reference to community; even more, it expresses a profound rejection of the collective and historical relative to her already mentioned "liberal" fear of totalitarianism. Her perspective is manifest, for example, in her "reading" of American History as a collection of events led or enacted by particular citizens who come together in social movements but remain as individual agents. Her individualism is an assertion that:

> The struggle is to do what our revolutionary forebears did during the early days of the American Revolution; what slaves and abolitionists did during the . . . struggles of the civil war; what working men and women did as they fought for decent wages . . . ; what the ancestors of slaves and many American young people, including feminists, did in the 1960's. In all these cases, it is the individual who is the basic unit of action even as the ideal of politics is a participatory one.[21]

The public space is conceptualized by Elshtain as completely devoid of moral values.[22] Women, again in the old terms of the dominant discourse, are in a position of privilege for bringing moral values—which seem to be exclusively in the family realm—to the public. Here, once more, I find Elshtain caught in the dominant politics of representation with the illusion of the private as autonomous and menaced by the attempts of "feminists" to reclaim the public.

BEGINNING TO THEORIZE

The Tension Woman–Women

Given limited and inadequate theories, and seeking to further theorize the question of the private and public, I analyzed a diversity of works with constant inquiry. My explicit intention was to restructure the terms in which public and private had been set and reclaim the public for women too. Soon, I became aware of the certain "naivete" of my approach. The statement of Judith Butler—on which I had reflected in a previous work—struck me once more:

> It is not enough to inquire into how women might become more fully represented in language and politics. Feminist critique ought also to understand how the category of "women," the subject of feminism, is produced and restrained by the very structures of power through which emancipation is sought.[23]

Thinking within the terms of "reclaiming the public for women," I was trapped in the position of accepting public and private spheres as given. The issue became, therefore, to analyze the common sense understanding of the private-public split, clarify the construction of the subject supposed to inhabit those spaces, and try to break through the structures of power of this limited theorization. Reflecting particularly on two problematic points—first, the consideration of the private and public as two substantially different spheres; and second, the identification of the subject that is supposed to inhabit them—what became apparent to me was the tension Woman-women as the subject of feminism. In this way, I decided to move my analysis of the private-public split towards a wider framework of discussion, the construction of the subject of feminism: the tension Woman-women.

In the dominant ideology, women are supposed to inhabit the private space, or be relegated to it, and men are supposed to inhabit/dominate the public one.

- How are public and private being conceptualized within this position?
- Is it Woman or women who inhabit the private?
- How does the tension between public/political and private/personal work on the background of macro-politics/abstract and micro-politics/experiential?

When writing a paper in which I was confronted with the statement that I was using a male discourse, leaving my body out, I became aware of the tyranny of the category Woman. Now, I not only saw how I was caught in the binary structures on which the discursive power of patriarchy is built, but I also saw how I was positioned as Woman, "the representation of an essence inherent in all women" while the material conditions of my writing, my own body, were completely ignored.[24]

The politics of the tension Woman-women is being powerfully recognized in many works such as those of Gayatri Spivak, Susan Jarratt, and Teresa De Lauretis, opening a space where agency and contestation are possible.[25] Teresa De Lauretis points out:

> . . . the discrepancy, the tension, and the constant slippage between
> Woman as representation, as the object and the very condition of rep-
> resentation and, on the other hand, women as historical beings, sub-
> jects of 'real relations' . . . women are both inside and outside gender,
> at once within and without representation.[26]

I can certainly relate this to the movement of the Mothers in Argentina who,
being relegated to the transhistorical role of guardians of the order of life within
the home, overflowed the restriction of such representation and engaged in a
political process that started with the defense of their children's life, continued
with the denunciation of state repression and terrorism, and reached the peak of
reclaiming democracy.

It seems to me that even while feminism as a plural movement made an
important turn to recognize differences within women, there is still a strong tendency to fall back into the question of Woman as its main subject. This determines many times the impossibility of recognizing the multiplicity and flexibility with which women enact roles that have been essentially defined. That is
to say, only engaging the paradigm of Woman does not allow one to perceive
actual women acting in concrete social, historical, and cultural settings.

If we—feminists—persist in concentrating on Woman (an essentialist position, indeed) we might even accuse the Mothers for politicizing their role as
such. Or, even more, we might blame them for not stepping outside their subject
positions as mothers to enter the public space to enact a more abstract and universal conception of citizenship, which some readings of the Mothers' movement
had done. If feminists just see Woman, not women in concrete social relations, we
lose sight of differences and get caught in the dead end of a binary opposition, not
able to articulate, as De Lauretis states, "the differences of women from
Woman . . . or, perhaps more exactly, the differences within women."[27]

Coming back to the dichotomy of private-public, it seems to me that the
woman that has been relegated to the private—and this as apolitical—is not
"women," but rather Woman. I certainly agree with De Lauretis that all women
go through the process of becoming Woman, but, as she recognizes, we are not
just that, we are historical subjects. Furthermore, we/women are constituted
through multiple languages and cultural representations, we are subjects . . .

> . . . constituted in gender . . . though not by sexual difference alone . . .
> [subjects] en-gendered in the experiencing of race and class, as well as
> sexual, relations . . . [subjects] not unified but rather multiple, and
> not so much divided as contradicted.[28]

Therefore, it seems to me that we not only have to pay attention to Woman as
the one caught in the private, but also to Woman constituted through different

representations. Even further, we feminists have to see women overflowing those representations as concrete subjects acting within concrete social relations. This certainly problematizes the reductionism of private/female and public/male, offering the possibility of a different and more complex reading of the political, the politics of gender, and the politics of representation. It seems to me an important step in the process of contesting binary oppositions and flooding the limits of sexual difference. Within this framework, the private-public tension is constituted as a space of struggle over different meanings and representations, a historical construction that, from a feminist perspective, needs to move towards more egalitarian and fair forms, which are certainly multiple and subject to continuous reconstruction.

If certainly we should deconstruct and contest the specific power relations that work in the Law/Logos male and in Woman as a representation of an essence, we feminists should also consider that,

> The historical and social operation of the sexual differential exceeds the discursive identification of sexual difference.[29]

The public and the private are both part of an ideological process which is enacted in a specific space and time by concrete men and women.

The Micro-Macro . . . But Always Political

Another aspect I would like to consider is the question of private as micro and the public as macro. Richard Johnson states,

> . . . private forms are more concrete, and more particular in their scope of reference, public forms are more abstract but also apply over a more general range.[30]

My general perception is that, historically, more emphasis has been given to abstract and collective forms of political action, while more concrete and circumscribed social action, which has also tended to contest and transform social structures, has not been recognized, not even studied. In terms of the specific power relations at work in the current sex-gender system, women's political action has been mostly concrete and particular. For example, women's grassroots political actions are organized around issues such as housing, child care, and health care.

My position is that we—feminists—not only have to stress the need to recognize the personal as political, but also demand the reconstruction of politics as an overflowing of the traditional model of intelligibility which conceives it as "the activities of elected officials and the working of government, both out of the reach of ordinary people."[31] If politics is perceived as the dealings of "elected officials" and "the working of government" no wonder that we will continue to listen to voices of women who say:

- We do not do politics, we just ask for our rights! (Interview with a woman in a shanty town of Chile in a TV program.)
- We do not defend ideologies; we defend life . . . Our great concern is not to be manipulated by any political party.[32]
- Our movement is not one of women who have extra time for charitable activities.[33]

This points out to me the need not to redefine politics in terms of the public, as rational negotiation, institutionalized practices, or in terms of the regulation by the state, or by referring to political parties and the struggle for public power. Political practices should go beyond these limits and be recognized in the ". . . content, values, symbols, myths, and rituals which women have developed in the course of their existence in society . . . ," in the ways these are controlled, used, and operate to resist and oppose.[34]

In the case of the Mothers in Argentina, for example, Feijoo points out their capacity to recreate the cultural dimension of politics by developing new forms of mobilization. Following Butler, I would stress much more the subverting power of these new forms by making explicit how these women took the rituals of the normative performativity games of being mothers, and pushed them to a point where they flooded the regulatory practices and became totally menacing to the intelligibility models held by the Military. As a consequence of this, many of the Mothers disappeared, others were kidnapped and battered, but they persisted. I would say, as they should have (as mothers, I mean). Why did not the father expect this, since the Army had positioned women as the guardians of their children?

I try not to be ironic, but there is still rage and pain circulating; as an Argentinean I also knew people that disappeared, and had a very close friend who survived detention.

Let us return to what I see as subverting forms. Furthermore, I would also add that I see these forms as pedagogical in the sense that they constitute meaning-making practices that deliberately take up assigned meanings and overflow them by offering emancipatory alternatives such as walking around the Plaza each Thursday at the same time to protest the disappearances. Is not this a doer "becoming" from doing, a subject that is not pregiven but rather recreates herself through collective action?[35] For me, the Mothers were mimicking the untiring woman that moves around the whole day and who has an established schedule for the laundry or the shopping. Another example is the handkerchief covering the head, something that traditionally—about twenty years ago—no woman would forget when going out of the house. In this case, the Mothers chose a white handkerchief—naivete, purity, passivity? Some of the mothers even painted on the handkerchieves the names of their children. They also took the family pictures, traditionally kept in the home, and displayed them on walls of the city, wore them as pins, carried silhouettes; creating a proliferation of concrete faces mingled with their own voices to counter the attempted 'non-identity' of suffering.[36] By doing this, the Mothers articulated an alternate discourse that not only bonded them, but allowed them to participate in collective action. In this way, the Mothers provided a different model of femininity and displaced the one portrayed as the "real"—showing it to be constructed—opening the possibility of an ongoing strategy. The previous normative model, even when giving women a central position representing them as moral guardians of society, was subjected to 'immutable laws' that established its qualities once and for all. Women were, therefore, objects of history, not subjects. The new model, the subverting of this naturalism and moralism of motherhood, seems to me to have stepped into the public making life and love political. That is, through the Mothers' action "The state is accused of corruption for observing neither the law of nature nor its own law."[37]

About Concrete Pedagogical Practices

The Mothers' movement served a much needed pedagogical function offering not only a critical and alternate paradigm, but also a space to unlearn oppression.[38] Many women in the country came to consciousness and reclaimed, along with their children, their participation, their voices, their anger. By asking for their children, they reclaimed life and love, they opposed the state of terror, and they finally challenged the regime. Feijoo states:

> . . . the defense of life and of the right to love . . . became a new feminist paradigm, sustaining the need for a feminine perspective in the world of patriarchal and masculine politics and suggesting a broader vision capable of destroying the traditional rules of the political game.[39]

That is, the Mothers' engaged in emancipatory pedagogical practices in the sense that they purposefully worked to challenge and transform not only the notions of truth imposed by the normative discourse of the Military regime, but also the subordinated and apolitical subject positions to which they have been assigned. In this progressive movement of unlearning oppression, they started around the limited step of demanding that their children were brought back alive. In doing so, they began articulating a political discourse that strengthened solidarity and launched them into evergrowing concerns for the disarticulation of the dictatorial regime and the re-establishment of democracy. Undoubtedly, these women enacted a pedagogical practice in the form of a counter-discourse inscribed in fundamental democratic values.

BEYOND HABERMAS' READING
OF THE BOURGEOIS PUBLIC SPHERE:
DEMOCRACY, MULTIPLICITY, AND THE PUBLIC

Having analyzed the concrete actions of the Mothers' movement, and considering it an example of a counterpublic sphere, I will now move to a series of final reflections on the concept of (feminist) public spheres. For this purpose, I draw heavily on the writings of Nancy Fraser and Iris Young. The writings of Fraser and Young provide a detailed and critically subversive analysis of the bourgeois understanding of the public sphere, deepening the radical possibilities of the Habermasian category. Therefore, I consider some of the most powerful conceptualizations and show the ways they are significant for me in terms of more democratic political and pedagogical practices in general, and the women's movement in particular.

First, it seems fundamental for me not only to discuss that private and public are both political and overlapping—as I already did—but to narrow further the category of the public into a more precise definition that shows its emancipatory possibilities for women and other oppressed groups. For this, we need to distinguish the concept of public sphere from a general understanding of the public realm. Fraser points out that many feminists have problematically conflated within what is public such diverse spaces as "the state, the official economy of paid employment, and arenas of public discourse."[40] She succeeds in demonstrating that this has practical consequences, rather than just being a theoretical issue.

> When agitational campaigns against misogynist cultural representations are confounded with programs for state censorship, or when struggles to deprivatize housework and child care are equated with their commodification. In both cases, the result is to occlude the question whether to subject gender to the logic of the market or the administrative state is to promote the liberation of women.[41]

The distinction within the public of what does truly offer a democratic space of participation and popular sovereignty seems to me fundamental. This close analysis prevents one from falling into easy binary oppositions and dangerous conflations that foreclose a deeper analysis to interrogate current institutional orders and open the possibility for their transformation. Jean Bethke

Elshtain falls into this trap when she rejects the deprivatization of child care as if that automatically implied its control by the state.

As a point of departure for further analysis and problematization, therefore, it is worth quoting Nancy Fraser's specification of Habermas's concept of the public sphere as:

> . . . a theater in modern societies in which political participation is enacted through the medium of talk. It is the space in which citizens deliberate about their common affairs, hence, an institutionalized arena of discursive interaction.[42]

As such, the public sphere is distinct from both the economy and the state in that it can be critical of them and offer alternate and transformative institutional forms.

About Problematic Assumptions

Habermas's account of the liberal model of the bourgeois public sphere presents problematic assumptions he did not take into account. I concentrate on two of those assumptions that offer an important insight into my previous analysis of the public-private split.

The first assumption refers to the problematic belief that the ideal condition for the existence of a democratic order is only one encompassing public sphere, and that "the proliferation of a multiplicity of competing publics" means a departure from it.[43] This assumption underlies the conception of the bourgeois public sphere and Fraser states that Habermas, rather than moving away from it, stuck to it as a principle. This pervasive idea of unity seems to me to be a burdensome heritage of modernist grand narratives still marginalizing those groups that do not resemble 'universal categories.' In criticizing this phenomenon, Iris Young follows Adorno's logic of identity, which she successfully compares with Derrida's critique of a metaphysics of presence. She states,

> The logic of identity tends to conceptualize entities in terms of substance rather than process or relation . . . [it] denies or represses difference. Difference . . . names both the play of concrete events and the shifting differentiation on which signification depends . . . The logic of identity flees from the sensuous particularity of experience, with its ambiguities, and seeks to generate stable categories.[44]

I find her appraisal powerful since she provides a language for the process I have concentrated on throughout this work. For example, I have been trying to move the categories of public-private from the designation of substances to the naming of shifting relations. Furthermore, I have been trying to overflow those categories by concentrating on "the play of concrete events" in the analysis of the Mothers' movement. Undoubtedly, the logic of identity belongs to a different language, one that is blind to action and experience.

Returning to the idea of multiplicity of public spheres, it seems to me that since inequality permeates spaces of deliberation in stratified societies, the existence of diverse public spheres, rather than a unified and comprehensive sphere, provides the conditions for subordinate groups to articulate their needs and discourses, widening the possibilities of a more radical democratic order.

An aspect I would like to consider within the question of multiplicity of public spheres is the pedagogical possibilities they offer as "training grounds for agitational activities directed toward wider publics" and also as spaces where the identities, needs, and discourses of the different social groups can be articulated in a process of collective empowerment that allows them to reflect about their experience and situation within the wider society.[45] In this way, pedagogical practices provide an alternate moral discourse that uncovers domination and oppression while encouraging the construction of more emancipatory social identities. Certainly, the Mothers have been/are an important factor in the democratization of the public in Argentina and a source of inspiration for other counterpublics such as diverse students movements, the renovation of political parties, or the radicalization of certain groups within them such as women's associations, official institutions, and others.

The Mothers in Argentina came together as private individuals seeking their children, and they ended articulating a discourse that moved them beyond these immediate concerns, constructing them as political subjects that actively denounced authoritarian rule and reclaimed a democratic order. Once in democracy, the Mothers remained as a subaltern counterpublic, rejecting all attempts of the government to incorporate them, or rather to coopt them. Many readings of the Mothers group see their action as a dead end in that it remains oppositional, not transforming itself to be able to widen its influence. In the context of Argentina's political history of fifty years of short periods of democracy in between ongoing Military Dictatorship, it seems to me that it is very difficult to work a political strategy that goes beyond opposition. Within a newborn democratic order, the transition to a democratic political culture is not automatic. Authoritarian practices and thought are strongly rooted, and emancipatory activities are perceived as menacingly subversive. There is a tendency to think also that democracy is reduced to the act of voting, and public accountability to the constituency is a remote aspect to be taken into account. The latter phenomenon became obvious when in December 1990, despite the opposition of almost 70 percent of the population, President Carlos Menem granted Presidential Pardon to the military commanders condemned by the Courts for the tortures, disappearances, and killings committed during the Dictatorship. This event, having taken place in the seventh year of democratic government, seems to me to stress the need for groups like the Mothers to keep the oppositional and contestatory stand while seeking other strategies. Contrary to the slogan launched by the government's conciliatory discourse, forgetting the past offers no exit to the future. For me, the recreation of a process of continual remembrance of the past problems in the form of an ongoing oppositional contestation is fundamental in order to prevent their dismissal.

The importance of respecting difference and plurality in democracy is that subordinate groups can develop their voices and articulate their needs if they have their own spaces rather than if they are absorbed in a consensual overarching public sphere. This issue clarifies the key role of the Mothers and other social movements rejecting their inclusion into the official space of party politics. Rather than the decline and fragmentation of the public sphere this should be seen as a healthy sign of political action.

Reflecting on the different stages of the Mothers' movement and recognizing the empowering effect their activities had, I reach a point where I wonder about the limitations it obviously suffered when—trying to be more than an opinion formation group—the Mothers struggled for some way to influence policymaking. They had refused to join party politics because, as they said, they did not want 'to be manipulated.' But, at the same time, party politics seemed to be the only articulated and legitimized channel within the new democratic order that provided access to state politics. I know that some of the Mothers, in a personal decision, joined political parties. Nevertheless, the movement has always remained independent in its organization. Questions arise such as: what institutional arrangements could offer social movements, such as the Mothers, the possibility to influence decisionmaking at the state level without having to be subsumed into party politics? In what ways can representative democracy be held more accountable when fundamental decisions, such as the Presidential Pardon in 1990, are made?

At this point, it seems fundamental to me to raise questions about the distinction between public spheres as mere opinion formation spaces and public spheres as also spaces of decision making. Nancy Fraser uses the categories of weak publics and strong publics to designate them respectively. She offers an important perspective when she distinguishes sovereign parliaments as strong publics, since they are "a locus of public deliberation culminating in legally binding decisions (or law)."[46] The question becomes: up to which point is the parliament really representative of the will of its constituency in an era when the distance between them is rapidly increasing. Fraser also considers the existence of strong publics in self-managed institutions such as child care centers, particular workplaces, etc.

Iris young addresses also the problematic of opinion formation and decisionmaking within democratic publics calling for institutional mechanisms and public resources to guarantee,

. . . group analysis and group generation of policy proposals in institutionalized contexts where decisionmakers are obliged to show that
their deliberations have taken group perspectives into consideration;
and group veto power regarding specific policies that affect a group
directly, such as reproductive rights policy for women, or land use policy for Indian reservations.[47]

What seems fundamental to me in the distinctions these theorizations create, is that an empowering dynamic of interlocking circles of accountability
develops, involving not only people directly linked to the institution in turn, but
also those indirectly affected by its workings. Furthermore, this process of
group deliberation and group generation of policy proposals is a fundamentally
pedagogical one in the sense that it constitutes a space in which people come to
consciousness, deliberately transforming not only knowledge about themselves
and their reality, but also transforming their own subjectivities.

The second assumption I would like to consider refers to the belief that
"discourse in public spheres should be restricted to deliberation about the common good," private interests and issues not having room within these terms.[48]
Fraser introduces here an interesting analysis of the underlying senses of publicity in play within this assumption, an analysis that clarifies my constant
inquiry around the politics of the criteria for determining what is public and
what is private. The sense of publicity that seems to me particularly enlighten-
ing is the one that considers public "of concern to everyone." Fraser states:

> The point is that there are no naturally given, a priori boundaries here.
> What will count as a matter of common concern will be decided pre-
> cisely through discursive contestation . . . democratic publicity
> requires positive guarantees of opportunities for minorities to con-
> vince others that what in the past was not public in the sense of being
> a matter of common concern should now become so.[49]

She illustrates this assertion with the powerful example of how the feminist
movement succeeded in transforming the vie of domestic violence against
women from a privatist perception to a matter of public concern through reconceptualizing it as "a widespread systemic feature of male-dominated societies."[50] In this way, this theorization sets the conditions for going beyond both
the liberal-individualistic and the civic republican conceptions of the public in
that it resists not only the idea of pre-given interests and needs around which
people reunite, but also the all-encompassing "we." Interests and needs get
clarified and constituted through deliberation and action. The outcome of deliberation can never be known in advance. The outcome might be a common
good or it might not. Therefore, so considered private or personal interests

should not be dismissed from public deliberation as the assumption underlying the bourgeois public sphere makes believe. Furthermore, in stratified or multicultural societies there is no way to frame deliberation within an all-encompassing and pre-given "we." The danger of making violence to subordinate groups is too obvious. The "we" and "common concern" of those who control dominant discourse and the rules of the game within deliberation might not certainly be the "we" and "common concern" of those on the margin or subordinate positions.

Iris Young also builds on this line of thought by arguing how current definitions of the public exclude from it most of the particular aspects of persons, such as gender, race, sexual preference, age, and depoliticizing citizenship.[51] On these terms, it seems to me that the traditional division between reason/body gets perpetuated, having oppressive effects.

It is clear to me that what is public and what is private is not just about difference but rather is part of the tension of a power struggle among diverse groups around multiple concerns and needs. Fraser powerfully states,

These terms [private/public] . . . are not simply straightforward designation of societal spheres; they are cultural classifications and rhetorical labels.[52]

I would add, classification and labels are used to legitimize some concerns for public debate and deligitimize others, serving the interest of multiple groups engaged in a power struggle for domination and control.

Returning to the work of the Mothers in Argentina, my source of practical reflection, I can recall how the democratic government tried to reformulate the Mothers' concern for democracy, human rights, and justice back into a private question. By working on the identification of the bodies of the disappeared—as if just that were the Mothers' claim—the government tried to end the Mothers movement. This was a reductionist move that framed their objectives to simply a matter of concern for their particular children. As a consequence, the Mothers' movement split. One faction remained radical in its work for democracy and justice. The other accepted being reduced to the 'pseudo-private' concern of having their children identified and buried or, in the absence of the bodies, finally declared as disappeared forever.

THE UNFINISHED PROCESS OF ALL THEORIZING:
IN SEARCH OF A DISCOURSE

When engaging in a dynamic of critical analysis, one always runs the risk of starting to reconceptualize without being aware of who we are and where we are positioning ourselves in the process. We also find ourselves using a language that not only does not reflect reality in an unmediated way but, on the contrary, constructs and represents life in a form that embodies the entangled relationships of knowledge and power. By engaging in such broad issues as pedagogy, feminism, democracy, and discourse I am trying not only to consciously position myself within a discourse of critique and possibility, but also to construct myself as a concrete political subject that struggles to make sense of the place and history in which I find myself.

By reflecting on the practices of a social group like the Mothers in Argentina, concrete historical subjects acting within concrete social relations and cultural settings, I perceived how dominant models of intelligibility of the private/public were overflowed, setting the conditions for a new discourse to emerge, springing from practice and, at the same time, transforming practice. From a more theoretical angle, it seems to me that by recovering the perception of women at once "within and without representation," the contradictions and overlapping binary oppositions become flooded, contested, and dispersed, giving way to the recognition of a politics of subversion and transformation.[53] If we—feminists—fail to develop this reading of "reality," we will remain tied to discursive practices and models of understanding that obscure the action of concrete women in their everyday life struggle. There is no way to keep the "control" of sanctioned politics when we begin to listen to the multiplicity of voices and see the diversity of practices. The consideration of the micro, the experiential, opens the possibility for a reading of dichotomies such as private/public as partial texts for engagement and transformation.

In this way, the purpose of this chapter is to develop an analysis of the dominant politics of representation of the private-public split by exercising the discursive possibilities of a feminist public sphere. Rather than beginning with a process of reconceptualization, the first step I took was to do a "reading" of the politics at work in the dominant models of intelligibility, identifying what was being placed at the center, as dominant, and what was being placed in the margins. But doing this reading implied having a language, a language of critique that operated as a framework that situated me/us within the world. The language I chose is quite an encompassing discourse that combines the traditions of radical democracy, feminism, and critical pedagogy.

4

Re-Creating Counterpublic Spheres:
The Mothers' Movement in Argentina
at the End of the Century

In the previous chapter, I extended my analysis about the Mothers' movement within the terms of how they served a pedagogical function, offering not only a critical and alternate vision of the situation in the country, but also a space to disarticulate oppression. The Mothers endured a hard and long journey to unlearn oppression, a journey that started when their children disappeared. As they say, "We were given birth by our children." They came to consciousness and turned into political actors through their children.

During the progressive movement of unlearning oppression, the Mothers began with the limited step of demanding that their children be brought back to life. In doing so, they began articulating a political discourse that, at the same time strengthened solidarity, and launched them into evergrowing concerns for the disarticulation of the dictatorial regime and the re-establishment of democracy. These women enacted a pedagogical practice in the form of a counter-discourse inscribed in fundamental democratic values.

The questions today, eighteen years later, are: What is the role of the Mothers in the context of a third period of constitutional government? How do they conceive their work today? How does the 'general public' perceive them? In which way have the conditions of the democratic culture in the country evolved, or not?[1]

These, and other related questions, were the core of a dialogue I engaged in with the Mothers' group in the province of Neuquén during 1994.[2] Neuquén constitutes a particular 'radical' place in the context of the conservative climate in Argentina during the Military regime. It was awarded the name "The Province of the Human Rights" because it was the first place in the country where the APDH (Association for the Human Rights) had a representation (besides the main office in Buenos Aires, the capital of the country).

The aim of this chapter is to show how the Mothers' movement still constitutes today an active counterpublic sphere. The Mothers have progressively enlarged their political commitments and, today, they denounce and work against a multiplicity of oppressive situations. By both redefining and reaffirming their role as mothers, they have moved away from the traditional conception of individual families and motherhood in a way which implies not only a transformation of social relations but also the socialization of motherhood.

By transcribing portions of the dialogue I had with the Mothers, I intend to display their collective struggle over the years and into the present, rather than stress their individual testimonies. I encourage the reader to look for the collective commitment that leads them into complex situations wherein "traditional" politics collides with ethics.

The Mothers interviewed were Beba Mujica, Inés Ragni and Lolin Rigoni.

EIGHTEEN YEARS LATER:
WHAT KIND OF COUNTERDISCOURSES?

How do the Mothers see their role today in Argentina, 1994? How do they conceive of their role? What do they do?

INÉS RAGNI (I.R.): The Mothers of the Square from Neuquén, after 18 years of being in the struggle, believe that the role of the Mothers movement is the same, exactly. Yes, in the beginning it was very, very hard, for every one of us. Each of us was fighting for a child, and today we fight for the 30,000 that disappeared. I believe that the fight of the Mothers is the same because we still do not have justice. We have a so-called democratic government but the Mothers say it is a constitutional government because, although there are no disappearances like the ones during 1976 and 1977, the Police have too much power against the youth, abusing their authority if they find groups in a corner, or after a party has finished. Too much violence, like before, even if people do not disappear. Young people still get beaten, they are taken to the police station. So, we say, it is still something similar. Today, in Neuquén 1994, people do not disappear, they are not taken by masked men, but people suffer because there are poor health programs, people die when they get very sick and there is no possibility of being healed, hospitals conditions are worsening. There are no jobs, there is too much poverty. This is also a violation, an abuse of the human rights. Some people say that because there are no more disappeared people, things are right. But during the constitutional government of Alfonsin, in 1985, some people disappeared in the province of Neuquén who have still not appeared; they remain in the same conditions of disappearance as the other ones. There was one man who disappeared that was freed by the police during Christmas time, he got out of the Police car in the highway, and never went back home. He was an employee of the Local Government's House. There was another young man who disappeared, he was also an employee of the Government. Also a waiter who served coffee in the mornings to the Governor. So, many other cases have not been cleared up. The procedures are followed, and then everything comes to a dead end. Nobody knows who the responsible people were. And this is 1994.

Have the Mothers participated actively in denouncing these acts?

I.R.: Yes, the Mothers have participated because we believe that even if we cannot do anything to find the responsible persons, we can encourage people to denounce these acts. We help them do that because they are still afraid of doing it. Yesterday, we visited a school for adults where we were invited to give a talk (men had already undergone the Military Obligatory Service, women were homemakers and mothers of four or five children). We had a beautiful talk, but there were still some asking why the Mothers of the Square exist today. Why are they still "in the street" (meaning in the fight) in 1994? We always say that until we get an answer, until we get to know who took our children, we will continue in the street. Because we are looking for 30,000 disappeared people. They are still missing, and their killers are free. So, we want justice. Justice needs to be done for us to stop being in the Square, or at schools talking about human rights, talking about the torturers, about the Army—because it hurts some people that we talk in those terms about the Army, they do not like it. Including the current government, today, . . . they say this has already happened, it is part of the past, that we should go on, that there is no future if you do not let the past go. So, we say that first, we have to see what happened, and then, from there, build a future. We have to tell young people what happened, they should know. Yesterday there were some young people at the talk who asked what had happened. We felt a bit angry they were asking why we were still fighting. We have been in the street for eighteen years. How could they still ask about us? How come they do not know? So, we insist that people today do not disappear, they suffer another kind of violence. They do not have employment, they do not have anything to eat. Some people steal, but they do not have jobs. We do not justify robbery. These social problems are also a type of violence against people.

Could you give concrete examples of things you have done, actions you have taken?

I.R.: We are permanently attentive to different events that occur in case there is any we think we should intervene in. We listen to the radio, we read the newspapers, and we only get involved in a problem after the formal denouncement (at the established institutions) has been made by the family concerned. We do not want to step on the family's decisions and actions, we support them. We go to the radio, we prepare notes for the media. For example, the Carrasco case that has recently come out.[3] We have worked as Mothers with other organizations since the beginning. Helping them, giving ideas to the family. First, their son disappeared. We started 'knocking at different doors' (going to different official institutions) looking for answers. Nobody knew nothing.

BEBA MUJICA (B.M.): I am proud of belonging to the Mothers' movement, having intervened as we did. If we had not, I do not believe the case would have come out the way it did. Although it is a very slow procedure—because every day there is someone else to be interrogated. But one of the things we insist on is that someone is involved in the case, someone with a high position in the Army hierarchy, not just simple officials or soldiers. That is the reason it is so difficult to find the responsible people. The Army knows very well who it is. In the beginning, when the Carrasco family came to see us, we started making much 'noise,' we went everywhere, to lawyers, to the media, to the cities of Cutral-Co and Zapala. We went to every place we knew the Carrasco family went for information or help in order to support them. We were always insisting that the Army was guilty of the disappearance. We knew they had done it. Our rejection of the Army was always present.

I.R.: When the Carrasco case started (he was first reported missing), a person who we still cannot identify made a phone call to a Human Rights group and explained what was happening to a soldier named Carrasco. My husband works with this Human Rights group so we, the Mothers, started working with them. We suggested the Carrasco family come to Neuquén (the capital of the province) to formulate a public denouncement, and also to give a public conference in the presence of the media, the Mothers, different Human Rights groups, the television, the radio. They accepted. Mr. Carrasco said at that time that he would be glad if his son were at the Army base. He added that he would be worried if his son were somewhere else, if he had escaped (some versions then indicated that the soldier was a deserter).

B.M.: He had been convinced by the Army to believe his son had escaped. When Mr. Carrasco went to visit his child he was not there. He was told his son had run away. So, Mr. carrasco started looking for his son outside the base. But, of course, the soldier was in the base.

I.R.: We were astonished that Mr. Carrasco would still believe that his son was safer in the Army base than outside. I asked if I could interrupt the conference and intervene, and I said to Mr. Carrasco: "Please, do not be calm if your son is inside the Army base. You should be calm if he is outside. Because if he is inside the base you will find him dead." He was shaken by my words. Many people did not like what I said, even him. We insisted that the soldier had not ran away. I added, "Mr. Carrasco, you should ask the Army for your son. He is in the base. He has probably been beaten, who knows in what conditions he is in." Mr. Carrasco looked at us, turned his head down. He did not say a word.

After the media conference, which got lots of general public attention, he changed his attitude. When he was told his son had escaped, he had the holy idea to go to a judge to denounce the disappearance of his son. This had more public impact and also made the case more serious. Mr. Carrasco went to Buenos Aires and visited the Mothers in the Square. He has been very receptive to the Mothers since then. He even talked in public to the Mothers.

This case got attention abroad because the Mothers movement has connections with international organizations. When General Balsa (the person holding the highest hierarchical position in the Army in Argentina) visited the base in Zapala (where the events took place) we decided we should go there to support the family. There were so many Mothers in the base that it seemed a Mothers' public event. The media was there interviewing us. What called everybody's attention was that the Mothers were at an Army's base. We said we were there not because of the Army, because we rejected them. We were there to support the Carrasco family as we had done since the beginning. We were at the official event where Balsa gave a speech, but we were facing our backs to him. During the talk he gave to the families of all the soldiers in the base, he asked everybody who was not a family member to leave the place. He added that he was very happy to have come to Zapala, that it was very important the work he had come to do, and a proof of that was the presence of the mothers with 'white scarves' in the public event. Then, General Díaz approached one of the Mothers and told her not to leave because General Balsa wanted to greet us. After a discussion among us, we decided to leave because we did not want to be portrayed by the media talking with an Army official. We said to General Díaz that the Mothers had nothing to talk about with General Balsa. That we were there accompanying the Carrasco family. When the media in the capital of the country published that the Mothers had been with General Balsa, we published a note saying that that was not accurate.

In another case, the Mothers intervened on behalf of Pablo Ramirez, a young man killed by a policeman. The Mothers had participated in public demonstrations demanding justice, and also had written documents and gone to the Government demanding an answer to the problem of violence against the youth. We always say we do not demand for a single person, but for everybody in need of justice. We insist that the institution responsible for the crime (either the Army, or the Police) respond, not the single individual that committed the act. Because the command, the gun with which the crime was done, was given by the institution. So, the institution has to be punished. They have the order to shoot down black heads' (popular sectors of the population). These young people do not have jobs, cannot go to school or the university because they do not have money to pay. What can they do? They cannot be found standing on a side walk more than three times, because the Police pick them up or shoot them. For us, the responsibility belongs to the institution. Some policemen do not shoot, but they watch what happens and they say nothing.

Another case we intervened in was the case of a doctor working for a local university in a health program, and now working for a public hospital in the city. He is suing two of the Mothers individually, not the Mothers as a group, because of a note we sent. He used to work for a hospital in Córdoba, in a hierarchical position where he was in charge of signing death certificates of non-identified persons (the disappeared) everyday. Did it never occur to him why there were so many people dying everyday without proper identification? He did this during 1976/77. Those people were buried in San Vicente Cemetery in a collective tomb. This doctor answered the Mothers through the media saying that what he was doing was right. There was a particular big truck carrying all those bodies away before dawn. If that was 'normal,' why always before dawn in such a way? Why buried in the cemetery at night? Why unidentified bodies? There were many people that testified about these events. This doctor claims he was not called by the CONADEP (National Commission about the disappearance of persons) to testify, therefore he is innocent.[4] There was another doctor in the hospital that went by himself to CONADEP to give information. Why did not X go? Because he was collaborating with the orchestrated repression at that time. We, as Mothers, denounced this doctor because we think that a person like him should not be working for a public service.

We have intervened in cases like this one and in many different others. For example, we supported the claims of the fruit workers (employees of packing companies) and other issues we consider fair. Many people think we only claim for the disappeared, but we have learned—after losing our children—to defend everyone in need. Before this happened, many of us as mothers and homemakers never thought to participate in these type of events.

GOING PUBLIC: THE SOCIALIZATION OF MOTHERHOOD

I.R.: The two of us worked at home, I had a small store. I worked for the community and my children. Maybe some Mothers had participated in politics before, but the vast majority had not. Maybe a few were teachers, or professionals, but most of us were mothers and homemakers.

B.M.: Small groups of the Mothers' movement remain in the provinces—because many Mothers have stopped participating. In the beginning many collaborated. I do not understand why many Mothers have stopped coming. They get isolated, and then they do not come any more. In Neuquén we were about forty, now we are only four working permanently. There are some Mothers that come once in a while, maybe because they feel the need to participate in a particular event that we organize. I think there is a strong influence from their families to stop attending. Right at the moment we should have continued working, they stopped coming. Gradually they have stopped coming. I was in Buenos Aires working with the Mothers there when the Mothers' group was created in Neuquén. Before this organization was created here, some of the Mothers were already working with organizations of human rights, as families of the disappeared, and with the APDH (Association for the Human Rights). The movement of the Mothers is initiated as a movement of 'families' of the disappeared, because we did not know yet what had happened to our children. We started to organize in 1976. The repression had started long before, but it was harder since 1975–1976. In 1976 we were working as families of the disappeared, and in 1977 we organized as Mothers.

I.R.: Our group of Mothers, in Neuquén, was constituted by around forty mothers. More than forty disappeared in this area. Some of the Mothers died. Some of them are ill. One of the Mothers, for example, was very sick and the doctors told her to quit working with our group. But we think her family had something to do with it.

How do the Mothers change? What role did their husbands and other family members play?

I.R.: In my case, my husband works the same way I do. We have a son who had to comply with the obligatory Military Service right after my other son disappeared, so it was very hard for us. I would say that other family members just abandoned the group.

Why? Were they scared?

I.R.: We do not know. They said nothing. They left. I think if we organize a public event in a square, we expect each mother to bring with her twenty or thirty from her extended family.

B.M.: I would be glad with ten per mother.

I.R.: We go to the square and members of our extended family are not there (besides their other children, husbands). Friends do not go. I say that friends are the ones we have today, the ones we made during 1976–77, not the ones we had before. All of them left us. Maybe they thought they were coming to a home of 'guerrilla' members, left 'wingers' ('*zurdos*'), and all that.

Could it be they were afraid?

B.M.: Maybe there was some fear. I do not want to discard that possibility. But I think it was more indifference to what was going on. In any case, they did not visit us. They wanted to keep themselves safe.

I.R.: I think fear is a relative issue. In 1975, a young man disappeared in the neighbourhood where I live, in front of an Army base. He worked for YPF (State Oil Company) in Cutral-Co, it was one of the first disappearances of Cutral-Co. I was working then in a community club (formed by women), where we learned to cook (sauces, jam), and also to sew. From these activities we got some money to help a school, a local church. The mother of the man who disappeared belonged to the club. People in the neighbourhood started saying "he was caught with guns in his room," "the Police took him," "he was thrown from a plane in the nearby mountains." I was very sorry because I was a good friend of his mother. In a meeting in the club I told the other women I thought we had to visit Eugenia (the mother) to support her. They said we should not intervene in the family business. I thought they were wrong. It was not a private thing. A child was missing from her home. This was 1975.

Did not the members of the group see their activity as political in any sense?

I.R.: No, it was just a way to meet, to get entertained, to go out. We reunited in different houses. So, we did not go as a group to visit the mother. My husband and I did. We could do nothing. I was in charge at that time of a postal service for the community, without salary. The young man disappeared for months, nobody knew anything. It was a lie that the Police had found guns and pamphlets in his room (this was a common claim then). Later, he was taken to Neuquén's jail, and a priest managed to find him; he had been a student of the priest in a religious school. The priest wrote a note and sent it to the young man's parents through his brother. The parents went to look for him at the local jail, but their son had been transferred somewhere else. Then, they found out he was in another jail in a province in the north. The parents travelled there, helped by the bishop of Neuquén (De Nevares). This young man, in jail, managed to write letters through people that helped him. He sent them to the address of the postal service I was in charge of. We phoned the parents to tell them when a letter arrived. On 21 December 1976 he was freed. On December 23, my son disappeared. On the 24th, a sister of the young man was getting married and we were invited to the party. Before the party, we took the present for the wedding and did not say our son had disappeared. We promised to attend the party later, but we did not go. We did not want to worry them. The following day they found out about our son through the paper. All of them came home immediately, including their daughter. They could do nothing, but they were there. The same way my husband and I did with their son.

All the apparatus to make people disappear had been organized since 1974.

There is a book about the disappearances in our region called *Buscado* ("Looked for") written by Noemí Labrune, with complete detailed information. My husband worked twenty-four years in the Army base across the street of our house, he was an employee of the food service they had there which was run by a private business. In 1974 my husband quit his job there. That year, the son of the owner of the food service (who was a member of our extended family) used to help on weekends, and when Army people were there they usually talked about "La Escuelita" ("The Little School) being built. The son of the owner—this is narrated in the book I mentioned—asked one of those officers what "La Escuelita" was. That man answered that "La Escuelita" was a place where they were going to teach some people to talk. But this young man did not know at the time what the officer meant (a torture center).

In 1974, when students from the region came back to visit their parents from La Plata (where they were studying at the university) and joined in different houses, they talked about the disappearances. I was very curious and I wanted to know, but my son, the one that disappeared (a student of Architecture), used to say that I did not know who the disappeared were, so it was no case for me to know about it.

B.M.: But I think he did that not to worry you.

I.R.: But I read the papers, I knew about what the Police were doing in La Plata. I wanted to know what was happening. When Susana disappeared in June (Mujica's daughter), then Alicia, Jorge D. came (he also disappeared afterwards) and told me about another person disappearing, Chicato C. I did not know at the time the family he belonged to. I asked Jorge D. what was going on that so many people were disappearing, he must have thought I was stupid. But he did not say anything. At that time, I had no idea of what was happening in the country. In February 1976, before the coup, another young man disappeared in Neuquén. He was also a student at La Plata, a friend of my son and other students from Neuquén. I did not know his family either. The coup was in March. By July this student appeared in the jail of La Plata. On December 31st, 1976, he was brought to Neuquén by Captain F. and freed during the night at his parents' house. He arrived in Neuquén during the day, and since it was daylight he was taken to 'La Escuelita,' and then was freed during the night. While being in "La Escuelita" he found out about my son being detained there too, but he did not say anything when he got freed. My husband and I heard about this many years later. My son and him were blindfolded so they could see nothing. But this young man could hear my son's voice answering the guards' questions, and he recognized it.

B.M.: What could have been the relation between this young man's family and Cap. F. for him to free their son? All of us were reclaiming our children.

I.R.: None

B.M.: How do you know? Nobody told you. How could he do something like that?

I.R.: No, he did it to make the Army appear as behaving good.

B.M.: Did he do it just to pretend? Why did he bring just this man back?

I.R.: We do not know. Maybe it was Cap. F. who detained this student.

B.M.: How long was this student missing?

I.R.: From February to December.

B.M.: Was he always disappeared?

I.R.: He was disappeared up to July, then he was registered as being in jail.

B.M.: So, why did I not know? My daughter disappeared in June.

I.R.: We do not know. He felt very bad for a long time. Who knows the things he was told by this Captain. It took him a lot of time to recover. He is a beautiful young man.

I.R.: This is something we do not understand. Many times I read the papers and I knew the things that were going on in La Plata. More than four times I went there desperate because I was scared something could happen to my son. I was frightened for my son, it was the fear of a mother. But I was not afraid about the general situation.

B.M.: That was because nobody talked about it, the repression was absent from conversations, news was distorted, and nobody wanted to talk about this at their homes; they avoided the topic. For example, Oscar (I. Ragnis' son) was always very active and did not ignore the activity of the Army, but he did not want to talk about it at home, I don't know why.

Do you think that people that did not have children studying at the university were able to understand the repression that was going on?

B.M.: No. I think they did not. If not, how is it possible that people did not get alarmed? In my case, I cannot deny I knew what my daughter did. She was very involved with a group. She had a degree in political science, she was teaching at the University here. I was very worried. Even more so when the daughter of a family friend of ours left for Mexico in February 1976; her brother had already gone abroad. He was very active in a group and knew what was happening, and that he had to leave. This gave me the idea that something big was going on, and that the repression was important. Since January he was urging my daughter Susana to leave the country. But she did not want to. I told her to leave, too. But she wouldn't. She said that she was working for something she believed was fair. She never accepted my suggestions.

So, she did not know that what was happening was massive.

B.M.: Yes, she did. But she was clinging to what she was doing. Then, when Susana disappeared I talked about all this with my other daughter, Irene. She was working as a teacher in Villa La Angostura.

I.R.: Oscar was working at the University Students' Center. This immediately made you a marked person for the Police and the Army. I did not have any idea of the activity the students did there. Like the Students' Centers in secondary schools today. I thought they were part of the institution, so they were right. I did not worry about it. But for the Army, the Police, there were not such good things when they started the repression. For them this was bad. I would never think something could happen to him because of that.

B.M.: Of course, nobody would think. In my case, I suspected there could be some problem. But I never thought it would reach those levels. We could not know through the news about many cases in Neuquén. We knew about La Plata, Buenos Aires. The Government saw the students' activities as dangerous. Many university students were working with the people in the shanty towns. That was a very active period. The Army knew what was happening. Problems with the 'guerrilla' in Tucumán had already started. So, the Army included all the students in the 'guerrilla' problem. Therefore, the commands to face the problem included everybody that was active for something, a student, a professor. And then, they also kidnapped anybody. That is also true. They came into the houses and took everybody, old people, young people, children. They destroyed everything, they stole. After Susana disappeared, I sent Irene to Italy. She did not want to go. Actually, she left the following year after Susana disappeared.

I.R.: It is hard to believe that the Army could take people just because they were working in a shanty town, in a neighbourhood. When I used to read in the papers that the students disappeared massively in La Plata, I was afraid. I told my husband I was scared. When my son came to visit, I would tell him not to go back to La Plata. He would say no. I offered to make an effort, sell some of our things and send him abroad. He refused.

DEMOCRATIC CULTURE:
WHAT ARE ITS EVERYDAY LIFE'S FEATURES?

Do you think there is a democratic culture now after eleven years of democracy in the country? That people are more receptive to these kind of problems? That they keep a memory of what happened?

LOLIN RIGONI (L.R.): From what I appreciate, I would say there has not been a significant process of conscientization within people. We have not advanced much. On the other hand, there is an important group of very young people, a young generation, ages 15/18 years old, that is very active, that wants to know and dares to know. It may be because they did not live the 'terror' of the Regime, they have a strong interest to uncover 'things,' they want to find out. In the older generations, I would say that there is not such an interest, there is rather an attitude of "letting things stay the way they are." This is hard to accept. Of course, there are always exceptions. People that struggle a lot.

With respect to something we were talking before, about us not getting stuck in the search for our children, that is an issue we will maintain by reclaiming them alive in order to keep questioning the system. All the constitutional governments to come should remember this. We will maintain this while we exist, while somebody keeps alive our cause. If our children were taken alive, they should come back alive. If they are dead, they have to say who killed them. Then, we will accept their death.

Another important question to point out is that the military commanders were condemned by the Courts in a civil, oral and public trial. All this was then 'swept' by the Presidential Pardon granted by President Menem in December 1990. We said at that time that his attitude was one of literally demolishing the people's moral trust in justice . . . We also say that the Presidential Pardon was an act of an individual man, an authoritarian one. But what we condemn more than the Presidential Pardon are the laws "*Obediencia Debida*" (Due Obedience), which exonerated military officers on the grounds that they were executing orders from a military superior, and the law of "*Punto Final*" (Full Stop), which established a time limit on the presentation of new prosecutions of military officers for human rights abuses. Those laws are worse because they were elaborated by legislators. Legislators are supposed to represent the people, and they raised their hands voting these laws. One legislator came to talk with the Mothers and said he would rather cut his hands off before voting these laws. Then he voted these laws, and he still has his hands . . .

B.M.: I also understand the issue of the democratic culture from this perspective. We live in Neuquén; it is a small town. In 1976 we practically knew everybody. Now there are more people, but there are only a few that join different social movements. I do not refer only to the Mothers. We support things done by other movements and organizations too [she mentions ATE, an association of state workers; ATEN, a teachers' association in Neuquén] when we believe that what they are doing is right. But there are many people in Neuquén, who I personally know, whom we never see at any event. I know they love me, they are my friends, but they never participate. In this sense, I do not think there has been any progress in terms of democratic culture.

I.R.: I do not call them friends any more.

B.M.: I agree. Sometimes I wonder if I could say "my friends" to some of them.

I.R.: I had a friend that I have not seen for many, many years, and she came to see me not long ago and she asked me when was I going to be at home, because I am out a lot. I told her to phone when she wanted to visit me because, as she probably knew, I had a moral obligation [meaning her work as a Mother]. She looked surprised and asked me if I was still busy with the Mothers. I got very angry when I heard this. How could she asked me if I was busy when I am looking for my son? This is a commitment for life. How could anybody ask such a thing? It is not the same thing when somebody died in a car accident. It is not like somebody disappearing and never knowing what happened. I told her to come to my home if she wanted, but that I was still 'busy with those things,' as she said. I added that I hoped she would never need me, because she has grown grandchildren.

B.M.: With respect to the question about the democratic culture, we see that these people have not changed, and the new members of the family continue to have the same attitude.

Would you call this attitude "a refusal to know?"

I.R.: Yes, these kind of people feel comfortable with the way they are and do not care about other people, although these 'other people' could be friends of theirs.

And at the wider level of the country, how do you see this democratic culture?

B.M.: We see it the same way. Maybe it could be a bit different in Buenos Aires. They still march there, and when we go to Buenos Aires we meet them in the square. But the Mothers there have suffered the same phenomenon of extended family and friends leaving the activities. I have a sister, she never came with me to any activity. But I know why, her husband prohibited her from attending any meeting with me.

"GIVEN BIRTH BY OUR CHILDREN": BECOMING POLITICAL SUBJECTS

B.M.: Hebe (de Bonafini) says we have been given birth by our children, because after our children disappeared we started to be conscious and to participate. It would have never occurred to me before to do what I am doing now.

The traditional role assigned to women was rather passive, restricted to the home . . . not to dare to confront.

I.R.: Yes, . . .

B.M.: But not everybody, Inés. Many in the capital of the country were different.

I.R.: Women before were destined to the home.

B.M.: In towns, yes. But in Buenos Aires women have been working outside the home for a long time.

I.R.: We do politics. Not party politics.

B.M.: That's why Hebe says we have been given birth by our children, because after what happened we opened our eyes and started seeing how the world of our children was. I was married with a man that was in politics (party politics). So, I knew about politics. My case is different than Inés (Ragni). In my house I always heard about everything that was going on. My two daughters were also very involved. So, I knew what Susana was doing. I cannot deny that. In Buenos Aires, when the Mothers group started, some of the Mothers belonged to different political parties. But we agreed that the Mothers group, as such, was apart from party politics. Mothers could belong individually to political parties, but this fact could never interfere with the activities of the Mothers group. It was accepted that no limit to the Mothers activities would come from party politics.

Did any political party try to attract the Mothers or any of its members individually to its activities?

LOLIN RIGONI (L.R.): . . . I tell you something: the Mothers, since the moment we socialized Motherhood, that we made ourselves the Mothers of 30,000 disappeared people, we knew that those 30,000 children belonged to different political parties, that they were from different ideologies, and some of them did not even belong to political parties. All of them were united around a desire of change, a desire to better the country, a marvellous solidarity that does not exist today. . . . With respect to political parties, some of them were *radicales* (Radical Party), *peronistas*, communists and else. . . . Therefore we have to be free, we should not to be restrained by belonging to any particular party, although individually we could sympathize with one. Our goal is different from the one we would pursue belonging to a political party. . . . Reaching our goal is going to take many years, we want to create in young people a consciousness of something new, different. Today *peronistas*, *radicales*, and others have no worth. Something new has to be born, with ethics, with solidarity; we have projects that might make a different life for our young people . . . Once we were criticized harshly because of our resistance to integration with political parties. We answered with an editorial article in the Mothers' paper entitled "The essence of our struggle" in which we explained that it is worthwhile to be ethical, to be honest, not like today . . . Somebody could ask how this could be done. We say we have to start from the wombs. Children should be raised in solidarity, in honesty. One day a political party will have to be born with these foundations . . . It will make of this country something different, but in the meantime . . .

B.M.: Hebe (de Bonafini) received invitations many times. She was even invited to be a representative for one party in the National Convention to reformulate the Constitution of the country (celebrated during May and June). It would have been great if she had accepted the invitation to the Convention. She's so prepared.

I.R.: Hebe said she was not prepared for that . . . Sometimes we talk among ourselves about the long journey we made from being homemakers to travelling to Europe representing the Mothers to contact international organizations. We never imagined this. We have met so many new people. Those are our friends. The ones we met looking for our children. When a traditional celebration comes like Christmas, Mother's day, New Year's Eve, who do we get to meet? Beba, my family, people working with us. I could never imagine myself in a TV program. I never imagined myself in a square with a microphone saying terrible things to an Army official. I cannot explain how could I do this.

B.M.: You had that inside. You have the strength to do that. I cannot do it. It takes a lot out of me.

I.R.: We were invited by a dentist to give a talk in a school in a neighborhood of a town named Covunco. This is mostly an Army town, since there is a military base there. We showed the movie *"La Noche de los Lápices"* ("The Night of the Pencils") about a group of secondary school students claiming cheaper bus fares for students, but are tortured and killed by the Army. A small group, but very integrated. A very nice experience. They had questions, they wanted to know. To give an example, if the school had eighty students, sixty were the children of Army families. But there were very few students. Mostly older people, and also teachers representing ATEN (a teachers' association of Neuquén).

THE GROUP'S HISTORY:
ABOUT SOLIDARITY AND COLLECTIVE MEMORIES

I.R.: Neuquén was declared the province of Human Rights because it was the first place where the APDH (Association for Human Rights) had a representation, and the mothers worked there as families of the disappeared. This commission was organized when the disappearances started in 1976. The Bishop,

Jaime de Nevares, and some families of a neighbor city, Cipolletti, thought something should be done. They started meeting in the church: Mr. Preiss and his wife, Noemí Labrune and her husband, a man from a Methodist church; we joined later. A group of "mad" people met, as many used to say. It was a wonderful group. We had already gone to see the Bishop because our son had disappeared. A friend of us went to the church to ask for a Mass for our son; the sister of the reverend told her to ask us to go there, to join the group in the Cathedral searching for information. This was January 1977, about fifteen days after our son disappeared. I told my husband, and I started going. We started visiting the families whose children also disappeared. We had a big group. It was incredible.

B.M.: It was a wonderful group. No doubt we deserved the name "Province of Human Rights."

I.R.: We had incredible meetings. We also had the first protest sign, even before the Mothers in Buenos Aires. About August 14, 1979 we had the first sign. We were twenty people holding the sign, in the corner of the Government House. The sign said "For Human Rights. Families of the Disappeared." The Governor was an Army man, Mr. Trimarco. We stayed in that corner, not knowing what could happen. Four people entered the Governor's house to present a document. One of them was my husband. What we did not know was that that day the Governor had invited for a barbecue people holding the highest hierarchical positions in the Army and the Police in the province. We were still in the middle of the worst repressive times. While we were there in the corner, we saw many cars filled with people from the Police and the Army. In the Governor's house there were many soldiers with guns pointing at us. All of a sudden, about eighty of them came to ask for our ID's. We saw people staring at us through the windows. Then we realized that they did not know what to do with us. We waited a long time for the four people that entered the Governor's house. They were not received by the Governor. Then we went to a newspaper's office to tell what we had done. The daughter of one of the families who was about thirteen then, was there in her school uniform. Her mother, who had entered the Governor's house, was terrified to see her there when she came out. She is a doctor today, working in a small town in the province. There was an anecdote, I had forgotten my ID. Since I was holding the sign, when the policeman asked me for the ID, I told him that I would tell him the ID number but I could not present the ID because my hands were busy. He accepted the excuse. I was not accustomed to carrying the ID with me. I was not even sure if I had given him the right number. If I had told him I did not have my ID, he would have detained me.

Are you being menaced today?

B.M.: No, we are not.

I.R.: Three years ago, an off-duty police officer killed a young man that said something to his wife. In a radio program I made a commentary of the event. I was very hard on the Police. When I got home two hours later, somebody phoned me from the Police to tell me that the Chief of Police wanted to talk with me. I thought it was a joke. He said the Chief wanted to see me the very next day at 10 AM. I told him to tell the Chief I worked, so I could not come. He asked me to hold on. Then the Chief came himself to the phone, and said he wanted to talk with me. He was very friendly. I said I had no problem. We finally agreed Saturday afternoon in his office. When my husband came, I told him about it. He wanted to come with me. I did not let him. When I went there that Saturday, I was wearing my white scarf. Everybody there looked at me with astonishment. We started talking, but he would not say why he had called me, so I told him what I thought: it was about me talking over the radio against the Police. Although he did not deny it, he said nothing. I told him I would never remain silent when cases like this occurred.

5

Taking Position within Discourse:
About Pedagogical and Political Struggles

... meanings are gained or lost through struggles in which what is at
stake is ultimately quite a lot more than either words or discourses.[1]

In this chapter I extend my analysis of the interplay of pedagogy, feminism,
democracy, and discourse to apply it to the re-thinking of pedagogical practices
within the university setting. In doing so, I concentrate upon the problematic
that emerges in the process of theory/discourse distribution and appropriation.
The ideas of pedagogy as counterdiscourse, and public sphere as a place for the
articulation of a multiplicity of counterdiscourses, are central to this discussion.

ON PARTICULAR PLACES AND CONCRETE PEDAGOGIES

Within education, most discourse that stands for theory about educational practice has been produced within a division of labour between
those who construct theory and those for whom it might have some
pragmatic value.[2]

Critical pedagogy works outside the inviolable boundaries of order, in
the rift between a subversive praxis and a concrete utopia . . . The
hope is that critical pedagogy rests with those educators who keep its
languages and practices alive while taking account of changing historical contexts and the specificity and limitations of difference.[3]

The multiplicity of discursive constructions within the university, the need to
historicize their production and contextualize their distribution in order to
assess their political and theoretical value, and the problematic gap between
those who construct theory and those who take it up call into question not only
a problematic division of labour, but also the processes of communication that
take place in the academy. In stating this, I want to point out the complexity of

the dynamic of knowledge production and the politics at work within it, and also the process, both pedagogical and political, through which this knowledge is distributed and appropriated. In this chapter, I concentrate on the particular problematic that emerges when educators—people mostly concentrated in the specific task of teaching and not so much in its theorizing—engage new theories and try to appropriate them for the transformation of their practices. This phenomenon is faced by teachers in general and particularly by those whose disciplinary field is not education, but who get involved in its theorization when working on projects of curriculum re-formulation in their areas. The particular discourse of critical pedagogy requires the bridging of the gap between theory and practice, envisioning an educator that can engage new languages and re-work her/his practice in an informed way. Within these terms, pedagogical discourse is removed from the discourse of methods and techniques, and curriculum theory is placed within the wider realm of social theory.[4] This approach not only redefines the problematic of theory and practice in different terms, but also creates the need for university intellectuals to engage these multiple discourses in a critical way. In addressing this problematic, there are two issues. First, there is a tangible gap between those who construct discourses and those who use them. This gap is organized around questions such as where theory is produced, from which position, and for whom (with their participation or not). Second, there are concrete barriers (in terms of ways of thinking and speaking) that make the reception and critical appropriation of discourses very difficult to those who do not produce them. For this reason, I frame the problematic neither around issues of clarity and verification, which are traditional hegemonic criteria that control the production of knowledge within the university setting, nor within the terms of particular anti-intellectual tendencies in the academy that dismiss theoretical work.[5] Rather, I concentrate on the communicative dynamic and the politics of the representational practices that take place when theory is distributed within the university setting. That is, I argue for the re-definition of the problematic of theory distribution and appropriation as a fundamentally pedagogical one. In doing so, I take up once again the task of remapping the linguistic, social, and theoretical boundaries between pedagogy, feminism, democracy, and discourse. Within this perspective, notions of the pedagogical are always political. Democracy and feminism, both in their particular most critical discourses organized around a politics of difference, can inform pedagogy with a specific project for social change. The following questions constitute the central components around which I develop my analysis:

- What does a politics of difference mean within the context of the university and how does it enable university intellectuals to develop a critical pedagogy?

- What particular pedagogical practices can be enacted within the university that would help re-work the gap between those who construct discourses and those who use them, or who work to apply them?
- How does feminism and the question of democratic struggle provide a particular political project to a pedagogy informed by a politics of difference?
- How can we conceive the university as both a weak and a strong public sphere?
- How do we link the question of the public sphere to the need to construct political subjects within the boundaries of the university and the university classroom?
- What is the importance of this particular critical pedagogy in our teaching, not only for our students, but for ourselves?
- How might this approach be taken up in a particular curriculum project?

In organizing this structure, my purpose is to highlight the aspects to take into account in the discussion, rather than answering the questions in a 'recipe' style. The issues raised are engaged as a whole in a critical analysis. Some times, suggestions and proposals are made; other times, I offer the terms within which the questions will remain as a constant reminder of problematics to be considered over and over

There is the need for a theory of language that takes up the question of a politics of difference, empowering professors to cross cultural, political, and theoretical borders. In rooting my work within a politics of difference, my purpose is to take into account both the diversity of particular struggles and the specificity of actions which suggest something about difference that makes it concrete, rather than abstract. And, in informing this politics of difference with a project of radical democracy, I provide the kind of articulating principles that would allow those various differences to come together in a common struggle. Therefore, one of the things that I want to argue is that a politics of difference needs an articulation such as democracy to allow those differences to form alliances and develop a common project. In chapter 1, for example, I provide a particular analysis of a politics of difference articulated within feminist pedagogy. In this specific context, women can translate private concerns into public issues and articulate their struggle with others in a wider democratic project. Within the particular institutional setting of the university, for example, a politics of difference calls on pedagogical practices to give voice to members of groups such as women, natives, and lesbians, and legitimize their stories and experiences in a dynamic that goes beyond a mere celebration or romanticization of difference.[6] That is, those stories and experiences should not be unproblematically accepted, rather they need to be seriously engaged, calling into question the oppressive social relations within which they emerged, and interrogating their particular content and form.

To talk about the university, is to talk about an institution that is involved in a process of certification and distribution of degrees: certifications and degrees that will enable those who hold them to apply for employment and get a position in the already organized job market. This fact puts the university in the position of either closely obeying the dictates of particular social and economic structures in terms of the curriculum to offer, or critically engaging those structures and contesting a reproductive role by developing transformative curriculums. Critical pedagogy addresses this problematic in terms of the kind of social relationships those curriculum legitimate, what and whose interests they serve, what contents and forms they make central and which they exclude, and how students are constituted within their practices. In taking up these issues, professors have to face their role as transformative intellectuals responsible for not abstracting pedagogical practices from wider social problematics and issues of public life. That is, within this framework the university represents an important public sphere in the sense that it constitutes a legitimate space for the analysis and discussion of those questions within the perspective of empowering counterdiscourses, as well as acting as a site for negotiation and policymaking. This approach places the role of the university professor in a critical perspective and redefines the university in a way that contests ". . . those ideologies and human capital theories that reduce the role of the university intellectuals to the status of industrial technicians and academic clerks whose political project or, lack of one, is often betrayed by claims to objectivity, certainty, and professionalism."[7] Within this type of discourse, curriculum needs to be analyzed as part of a wider set of relations where questions of content, disciplinary fields, teaching practices, and teacher-student relations intersect with issues of power and culture articulated along axes such as race, gender, class, sexual orientation, and religion. The language of democracy is the one that provides this pedagogical discourse with a political project that speaks for critical notions of citizenship and democratic community. That is, rather than defining the wider goal of the university in terms of making students critical thinkers, democracy narrows the scope pointing to the need for providing students with the opportunity to develop a sense of agency framed by ethical terms such as justice, solidarity, and community. This means to empower students not only in order to understand their positions, experiences, stories, and voices within the complexity of society, but also to be able to produce alternate responses that escape binary oppositions and contribute to the development of communities of solidarity. In taking up this approach, the university can play a fundamental role in enhancing more participatory forms of public life, providing a radical democratic vision of the future. That is, all those particular struggles that a politics of difference allows to emerge, can be articulated within the language of democracy with alliances built among themselves in an ongoing process of reformulation and transformation.

Re-defining the role of the university as a setting mainly concerned with processes of articulation and negotiation of counterdiscourses as well as the creation of public spaces of deliberation and policymaking, requires a complete change of direction from hegemonic conceptions of theory production and distribution. Within this new framework, notions of science as being objective and truth revealing are rejected and replaced by considerations of the historical and social conditions of knowledge production.[8] University intellectuals should go beyond traditional normalizing parameters of science, taking into account the partiality and contingency of all processes of theory production.[9] This creates a complete new relationship between theory and practice making apparent the politics of knowledge production. Within these terms, the gap between those who construct discourses and those who appropriate them can be re-defined in wider political and pedagogical terms. That is, there are multiple discourses articulated around different histories, languages, experiences, and cultures that need to be engaged, attending to ethical and political concerns. Within this problematic, I want to particularly address the question of the politics of knowledge distribution. By this, I mean processes such as the way knowledge is made available within the context of the university, the concrete dynamic enacted in its appropriation, and the criteria developed to regulate the construction of particular curriculum projects. As stated in the general introduction to the dissertation, the process of distribution of discourses is usually reduced to a mere dynamic of transmission, many times partial, where the text is supposed to speak for itself without taking into account the historicity of its production, the particular space and time of its appearance, the needs, problematics and location of the subjects involved in its development and those of the subjects involved in its appropriation. That is, discourses get fragmented, divested of the circumstances that nourished them, and finally distorted, void of any significant content to help name, conceptualize, and approach concrete circumstances in a critical and transformative way. In this reductionistic approach, theories lose power and become many times just fashionable discourses, trends to be followed because someone in a leading position points at them.[10] It seems to me that, taking into account this problematic as a whole, there are two aspects to consider. First, the lack of significant dialogue between those who construct discourses and those who engage them. And second, the poverty of the pedagogical practices enacted in the process of appropriation of discourses that reduce themselves to mere transmission processes. Considering the university as a fundamental public sphere in the sense of being a site for deliberation and, particularly, for the

negotiation and articulation of difference, there is the need to develop dia-
logical pedagogical forms that create communication between those who produce the discourses and those who attempt to take them up. This means not
only to avoid the colonizing effect of speaking for others, but also to recognize
that the access to theory demands from the subjects involved in the process the
rearticulation of their subjectivities. Discursive structures, when engaged, not
only require from the subject involved in the task the acquisition of a new language, but also the re-articulation of her/his subjectivity in the sense that those
structures offer a new referent from which to understand the world and themselves.[11] This question needs to be considered in its pedagogical dimension in
order to, on one hand, prevent the alienation of the subject involved in that
dynamic, reducing him/her to an object; and, on the other, empower him/her
by taking into account his/her location. That is, in the process of discourse distribution, there is the possibility of being politically correct, but pedagogi-
cally wrong. The consideration of all the aspects already mentioned calls for
critical pedagogies that attend to the necessary historicization of theory in
general, the curriculum field and concrete curriculum constructions in particular, and to the special needs, experiences, voices of those involved in the
process of their appropriation. A fundamental issue that these concrete pedagogies should take up is the need to conceptualize the appropriation of new
discourses as a process of learning languages; languages that allow not only
the access to different ways of thinking, but also to the reconceptualization of
problems and the discovery of new ones. Language constructs its object of
study, rather than reflecting it.[12] To acknowledge the problematic of language
means to take into account the displacing potential of theoretical discourse
upon those involved in the appropriation of knowledge.[13] Therefore, it is fundamental to create the conditions for generating dialogue between constructors
of discourses and those who appropriate them, contesting the oppressive hierarchical positions of subject-object relations, and enabling those involved in
the dynamic of appropriation to become subjects. I would like to stress that by
taking up the multiplicity of aspects mentioned, particular critical pedagogies are called for, not only for our students, but for ourselves: pedagogical
practices that have to pay attention to fundamental formative problematics in
both professors and students and, in doing so, organize the construction of particular curriculum projects in an ongoing process of critical engagement. This
approach emphasizes the need to construct political subjects out of university
intellectuals—both professors and students—capable of engaging wider social,
economic, and political structures as critical citizens. That is, it is fundamental
to consider the university as a key public sphere responsible for the formation
of citizens capable of participating in political struggles for social transformation outside the university setting, since the larger processes of knowledge
production and distribution are negotiated in the wider social context.

ABOUT SOCIAL VISION AND CLASSROOM PRACTICES:
A SITE OF STRUGGLE

The struggle is itself a condition basic to the realization of a process of pedagogy: it is a struggle that can never be won-or pedagogy stops.[14]

What does a critical pedagogical practice consist of? What can be done to contribute to form/constitute reflexive subjects with a critical attitude who are committed in their work towards social transformation?

When I pose the former question I am mostly thinking as a professor within the University setting involved in a program of Teacher Education. This implies both a look at the already organized professors' practices in order to engage them critically and transform them, and a look at students as future teachers so as to enable them to develop a critical pedagogical practice. This does not mean I do not take into account pedagogical practices within other institutional spaces outside the institution, but rather that my immediate concern is to reflect on those concrete activities that have to do with 'teaching those who will teach others' or 'forming those who will form others.'

In previous chapters, I deal with the process of constructing a transformative social vision articulated in a particular conception of the relation between theory and practice understood in terms of an emancipatory "praxis."

In this section, my aim is to develop both a set of criteria on critical pedagogy in 'action' and a reflexive recovery of concrete pedagogical practices that have already been enacted. All this in order to cover the gap/void usually existing between theoretical formulations and action proposals destined to guide the everyday practices of teachers as transformative intellectuals. By stating this, I am not placing myself within a prescriptive discourse which assumes that determined 'techniques' or 'methodologies' carry within/by themselves emancipatory possibilities which could be applied by anyone in any circumstance. Rather, I suggest that it is necessary to study the operative dimension of critical pedagogy, analyzing how particular practices are constituted and how they work. It is also important to step inside and outside the classroom when taking up this challenge. A critical pedagogical practice is an ongoing process that redefines itself constantly, taking into account both personal and social investments.

Recognizing within the pedagogical relation the tension teacher-knowledge-student, the present approach to the problematic—without implying a hierarchical order in the naming of its elements—will focus on the teachers/professors and student teachers end, since they are the ones to develop and apply alternative theories and methodologies that operate not only in the subjective conditions of education related to the question of what it means to be a teacher, but also in the objective conditions of the educational system. In the current historical juncture, the educational system is a problematic arena, a site of struggle among oppositional discourses in the light of the neoconservative "assault" on emancipatory pedagogies.[15]

The Tension Knowledge/Knowledges: School Knowledge

We must not simply speak of knowledge but of knowledges, since all knowledge is relational and can only be understood within the context of production, its distributions, and the way it is taken up or consumed by different individuals and groups . . . knowledges are invariably mutable, contingent, and partial; furthermore, their authority is always provisional as distinct from transcendental. Knowledges may, in fact, possess the power of truth but in reality they are historically contingent rather than inscribed by natural law; they emerge, in other words, out of social conventions and sometimes in opposition to them.[16]

In order to sketch out any consideration about action within the pedagogical realm, it seems fundamental to me to start analyzing the concept/s of knowledge we carry with us. Knowledge is the core of the pedagogical relation since pedagogy is about the production of knowledge and the constitution of subjects in the context of particular social relations.[17] Therefore, conceptions of knowledge turn into particular practices that constitute subjects to accept their place in society, conceiving it as "natural" or enable them to perceive oppression in its articulation through complex questions such as class, gender, race/ethnicity, and work to transform social relations; practices that, in the end, contribute to either transform or maintain the current social order.

McLaren dismantles naturalized conceptions of knowledge and approaches the complexity of the problematic through questions of production, distribution and reception coming out of work in cultural studies. In this way, he points out very clearly that knowledge is constructed in close connection with cultural context. That is to say, a context ridden by power relations where diversity of values and interests conflict over multiplicity of social and political concerns. Understood in critical terms, knowledge is not about a universal, transparent, and neutral body of cognitions, detached from the knower.[18] Taking into account some distinctions within the abstract concept of knowledge, it can be said that scientific knowledge, as a particular construction, is produced by a community of professionals who share certain discourses which establish the logics to follow, the questions to answer, and the methodologies to apply. This community responds to particular cultural and political concerns according to its location in the socio-historical context.[19]

From another perspective, school knowledge in the context of the critical approach does not constitute—as the hegemonic concept holds it—a standardized and rigid body detached from everyday life. School knowledge, as a particular selection and reconstruction of the wider scientific knowledge, should be demystified and its connection to cultural networks worked out. Students need to be recognized as knowers who come to the process of learning/knowledge appropriation, carrying their own experience, their own knowledges. The work of the teacher, as a transformative intellectual that struggles to control the conditions of it, consists of mediating the interplay of the multiplicity of knowledges, facilitating a critical reconstruction, "transpositions," distribution and appropriation.[20] The relation between scientific knowledge, school/academic knowledge, and students' knowledge is a fundamental and unavoidable discussion for following through in the process of reflecting on pedagogical practices. This discussion, as pointed out previously, is local, contextual, and temporary in the ongoing struggle of pedagogy.

Just an Epistemological Rupture?

Thinking about students as epistemic subjects that come to know in the concrete setting of the classroom brings us back to considering the different epistemological status of students' knowledges compared to scientific knowledge. Students' knowledge, understood within the Gramcian terms of common sense as contradictory conscience, is constituted by the sedimentation of diverse conceptions of the world articulated in a fragmented and dispersed way. These conceptions are developed in interaction with a classist social order but also, I would add, with a sexist and racist one.[21]

The work of the teacher comes into play as an intervention that has to bridge those knowledges, in the sense of working on the continuities and ruptures existing among them, articulating their dynamic/tension within the organization of school knowledge. From a critical perspective, school knowledge is the one that has to be selected and organized with the specific purpose of facilitating students' process of appropriation/construction as an active subject involved in the action of learning. The critical pedagogical practice is so in the sense that it legitimizes students' experiences, enabling them to both question and reconstruct them, to be the agents in producing an "epistemological rupture" by connecting their own ways of knowing with more systematic structures and dynamics in a larger cultural context. That is, from a critical perspective, students should not only accomplish an epistemological rupture in the sense of working on the reconstruction and systematization of the continuities and discontinuities among knowledges. They should also be able to "reconstitute" knowledges in close relation to the social order they inhabit.

But, how to do that? How to facilitate the process of epistemological rupture within the classroom? As I stated in the beginning, there cannot exist general abstract prescriptions for any situation since there is continuous contextual change and diversity of teaching spaces.

Reading Practices: Language and Experience

> What students need . . . from us now is the kind of knowledge and skill that will enable them to make sense of their worlds, to determine their own interests, both individual and collective, to see through the manipulations of all sorts of texts in all sorts of media and to express their own views in some appropriate manner.[22]

One way of approaching the dilemma stated in the previous section is to start by analyzing students' language, taking into account the categories they use to articulate their experiences. Language is the medium through which the world is represented, lived and experienced.

The first step may possibly consist of identifying the categories students' use in the context of the activities organized within the classroom. One of the routines students perform are reading assignments. Within the critical paradigm, reading is conceptualized as an integral process that does not reduce itself to the reproduction of the meanings the text carries. More than that, the subject produces new meanings and significations when connecting the text to her/his experience and to the wider cultural context, constructing another text.

The study and textualization of the categories, logics contained in this "new" text, the one the student produced, should uncover general assumptions about the world, society, women/men, education, revealing underlaying interests and values. Robert Scholes conceptualizes this process powerfully stating,

> We must help them [students] to see that every poem, play, and story is a text related to others, both verbal pre-texts and social sub-texts, and all manner of post-texts including their own responses, whether in speech, writing, or action.[23]

This approach illuminates the complexity of meaning production, pointing out how we "embody" it and act it within the context of the wider social order.

The systematic reconceptualization of categories enable not only progressive levels of theorization, but also a transformation of the representations which, in turn, will be acted out and will contribute to the process of personal and social transformation.

Exploring and Reflecting on Feminist Pedagogy's Practices

> The classroom is an ideal site for investigating how theory works, what languages it speaks, what claims it makes, what strategies it adopts.[24]

As I stated in the introduction to this section, my purpose was not only to develop some criteria to have as a referent when reflecting on critical pedagogical practices, but also to recover concrete experiences of those practices that could exemplify the kind of conflicts and situations a teacher/professor confronts when challenging hegemonic assumptions about the "classroom order."

Following a graduate seminar and a national conference (Feminist Sophistics, Miami University of Ohio, June 1990), seven women—six graduate students and a tenured professor—"formed a feminist pedagogy research group to pursue the relation between feminism and composition teaching . . . ;" ". . . we formed a collaborative inquiry group because we all consider ourselves feminists writing teachers committed to developing theories and practices of pedagogy responsive to gender and other differences: race, culture, class, and sexual preference."[25] The "object" of our study was Miami University's required first-semester writing course. Five of the members of the research group taught the course in the fall of 1990, the other two contributed to the reflection process. I was one of the two working ". . . in the collective process of reflecting and questioning our assumptions and conclusions . . . My particular question for our project concerned the relation between specific classroom experiences and the generalization demanded by theory."[26]

The work in this project was organized around a solid body of knowledge with no closure, always open to critical reformulations coming either from diverse theoretical perspectives—like cultural studies, critical pedagogy—or from the "knowledge" produced through the informed reflection over practice itself. This accounts for the impossibility of offering general abstract rules within the broad paradigm of critical theory. Rather, the challenge is to submit all practices and theoretical approaches to an ongoing critique to avoid rigidity and closure within a process of transformation. This constitutes a continuous challenge difficult to respond to.

One of the main assumptions that informed the organization of the class syllabus was that the classroom itself is considered a site of conflict in the sense that difference and power are articulated around issues such as ethnicity, sexual orientation, and others. Consequently, one focus of the analysis was the articulation of classism, racism, and sexism in language usage. A particular way of working these sources of conflict in the classroom setting was to ask students not only to connect their experience to social issues, but to locate themselves within the web of the relations of class, gender, race, and others. Susan Jarratt pointed out that ". . . naming their own social locations would ground their stories in socially specific, and thus more socially responsible, accounts of personal history."[27] She also mentioned how sharing with her students tools of sociolinguistic analysis meant that ". . . becoming a responsible language user demands an understanding of the ways language inscribes difference."[28] Informal response papers, journals, personal narrative assignments, workshop groups, writing assignments dealing with minority concerns, class readings setting forth radical views, and invited speakers, constitute an example of concrete strategies developed.

Many conclusions might be drawn from the group's accounts. It seems important to me to mention, among them, that conceiving the class as a site of conflict allowed for the recognition of tensions about race, gender, class and other differences demanding the development of a flexible practice, and legitimizing struggle as positive and productive. This means a pedagogical practice that is always in a process of re-articulation in terms of personal and social investments.

Checking a Curriculum

I have been reflecting on diversity of theoretical issues that constitute the core of a critical pedagogy and also reading certain practices through the lenses of this theoretical approach. But, what happens when we, as teachers, create a particular curriculum and organize activities following the lines of critical pedagogy thereby engaging students in its terms?

The purpose of this section is not to offer a detailed account of a course I taught following the lines of a critical approach, but rather to show some of the issues I posited and the questions I faced.

In Argentina, during the second semester of the academic year of 1994, I taught a course within a program of Teacher Education for students that would become Language teachers and Geography teachers for secondary level schools. The course, named "Education, Society and Politics," consisted of a global proposal that integrated a wide range of issues such as general pedagogical content; politics, legislation, and administration of education; an introduction to the educational reality of the country, its history of education and also fundamental questions concerning contemporary education. The complexity of the project implied an interdisciplinary approach.

Considering critical pedagogy as constituted by a close linkage between practices and content, I organized the curriculum of the course in a way that offered both a body of knowledge that would challenge common sense understanding on education, and a set of activities that would demand from the students the use of and reflection on the knowledge they carry and the production of their own texts.

I chose to approach the interplay among education, society and politics within the context of the processes of production/distribution and appropriation of knowledge, departing from the notion that pedagogical practices are complex social practices that produce, reproduce and transform knowledge and subjects within a particular set of social relations. This was supposed to consider both a subject engaged in the process of knowing, and a body of knowledge complex enough to include, for example, common sense as well as academic knowledge. The purpose of this curriculum was to provide a critical look at diversity of "reality constructions" conceiving disciplinary knowledge as a discourse that provides metaphors and images of the social world through the particular logic of the language used—which is always linked to political, economic and socio-historical relations that carry certain values and interests.

The macro idea that operated as a background to the axe constituted by the relation education/society/politics was the characteristics and possibilities of the processes of change within society. Change understood either as discontinuity, rupture or as evolution, continuity. In the end, the purpose was to perceive these processes in terms of the tension reproduction-transformation within the political, the economic and the ideological realms.

I organized the operative dimension of this pedagogical approach around a "critical reading practice" through which I invited the students not only to read the texts selected ("basic understanding"), but also to contextualize them ("interpretation"), and then reconstruct them ("re-write"). To understand reading while taking into account these dimensions, meant the students must consider themselves situated subjects, subjects belonging to a particular social group in terms of class, gender, and race/ethnicity; subjects that were capable of critical appropriation and transformation. Therefore, the challenge to the students was to situate themselves not merely as consumers but as subjects capable of producing new meanings (new texts).

I structured the content of the curriculum to include four bodies of knowledge that responded to the diversity of issues and disciplines the course approached. Each of these parts had its own internal logic that also responded to a wider rationality. The first part introduced the students to basic epistemological considerations and then to the fundamental conceptual categories with which the whole curriculum was organized.

With respect to the learning activities I organized, I departed from the assumption that the learning process supposes a series of moments that are not always considered in terms of the time required by the subject engaged in it to accomplish them. Usually, classroom activities responding to wider learning purposes are taken into account only in terms of themselves, not being understood in their relevance with respect to the rest of the curriculum. That is, certain activities which are organized to work with the content of the curriculum do have a short term purpose in themselves but also a larger one relative to the rest of the curriculum. This has to do with the way knowledge and knowing are conceived. The moments or phases of knowing as part of a continuity are not always recognized. There is usually the belief that learning and understanding occur all at once, and the sense that something is being constructed or re-elaborated gets lost. Therefore, the idea of process and time disappears. The concept of knowledge underlying these conceptions is that it is something packed, finished, compartmentalized, and not something that develops or is being constructed, where the subject that is engaged in its apprehension is active and takes part in its inaction. Knowledge is not a set of compartments, and knowing is not one fully accomplishable and expectable act. Both knowledge and knowing are a complex and never ending process that develop in particular social and historical contexts.

When I started teaching the course, I presented its curriculum with an introductory section designed to clarify some epistemological and theoretical issues, such as the diversity of ways to produce knowledge within the educational field (educational research), and the categories needed for a critical approach to education. The different sections of the program—a total of four—developed these categories within the chosen theoretical approach. Though the first section seemed rather abstract, it was presented to the students through activities in class that engaged their concrete perceptions of reality; also represented examples of situations where these epistemological/theoretical questions were at play and embodied in everyday life situations. The applied logic started with the abstract, then moved to the concrete, and returned to the abstract. The possible steps would be: first to present and study the conceptual categories with which to think reality—in the sense of "metaphors and images" provided by the language used—and to confront the idea that it is possible to approach the world and be neutral and objective perceiving it just the way it is. Next, to engage in the reading of the world using the categories selected. And finally, to reflect on the categories and the readings obtained comparing them with the readings done through common sense ways of thinking. Although there is a sequence in these moments, they are dialectically intertwined. My general strategy was to depart from the understanding that when we come to know something we have to reflect on how we know, and what knowledge is. These questions are inherent in education itself.

In order to assess the course and get the opinion of the students about the curriculum proposed, we had a collective evaluation at the end of the semester to discuss both the content and the methodology. I also interviewed a few students to get more precise information in order to write this section. The general response of the group to the curriculum was very encouraging. The students stated that it provided the structure—meaning the explicit logic that gave the curriculum its particular rationality—for understanding the content by introducing the basic epistemological and theoretical questions related to the process of knowing and the production of knowledge. They valued this approach very much because it revealed their own assumptions about knowledge and knowing. This particular curricula challenged their common sense representations relative to their apprehension of a new body of knowledge. In this way, they found themselves engaging critically the diversity of constructions of reality and appreciating the reading of the different texts instead of hearing teachers' summaries which represent only particular mediations through their particular lenses and readings of reality.

With respect to the moments or phases of learning, the students pointed out that the curriculum was apprehended as a totality at the end of the course. Each of the sections' internal logic was perceived as constituting part of a wider body of knowledge which, at the same time, involved a more comprehensive logic. That is, the curriculum as a "totality" with a particular rationality was finally reconstructed by the students individually through the work done during the semester as they produced their own readings and texts.

Some of the curriculum difficulties involved, for example, the complexity of the conceptual categories—such as civil society, the state, hegemony, and the work required to reconstruct them through the different sections of the curriculum. In the end, the students in general were able to experience the way the categories were gaining meaning by establishing a rich net of relations, many of which I had not been aware of. Another difficulty for the students was working with the categories class, gender, and ethnicity, and seeing themselves, for example, as gendered bodies in the classroom. The traditional subject involved in the process of knowing was supposed to be a neutral one. Although it was not an objective I formulated, it is a question I would like to develop in the future.

About the texts the students had to individually produce at the end of each of the four sections of the program, they stated that, although it was hard for them to "synthesize their readings" in a coherent way, the challenge to reflect and show their productions contributed very much to their ability to find/construct the relations among the different topics, to perceive them as a whole and, most of all, to read reality with critical lenses.

I appreciated very much the students' observations since they provided me with the elements I needed to keep working on the conception of the learning process and the strategy I developed to articulate the theory and practice of the course. Knowing and knowledge production is a never ending process, a totality that has no closure.

Conclusion

This section explored the possibility of concrete strategies to 'bring into life' critical pedagogical practices in order to delineate both a set of criteria on critical pedagogy in 'action' and a particular articulation of a reflexive theory 'at work.' All this, in the light of a logic that takes as a necessary step the study of the operative dimension of critical pedagogy to analyze how particular practices are constituted and how they work in order to guide the everyday practices of teachers as transformative intellectuals.

As I have already stated, pedagogy understood in these terms escapes any attempt of prescription or claim 'emanating' from a homogeneous body of theory. Some of the axes around which it works include: experience, difference, voice, conflict, power, and the collective. This approach demands a constant reflexive attitude towards its languages, its strategies, the social relations it legitimizes, and the voices it enables or silences. Such a attitude may open transformative possibilities for us all.

6

Conclusion

RECAPITULATING

Throughout this work I used the categories of pedagogy, democracy and discourse so that the three are bound to each other in a metonymic relationship. That is, I have connected each as a necessary part of the others and centered their meanings around the idea of a political imaginary of emancipation.[1] In this way, I argued for the value of placing pedagogy within a radical democratic language to provide it with a particular political project in order to not only articulate ourselves as subjects, but also to effect change both in ourselves and in the social world we live in. I stressed the importance of the realm of discourse as a means for creating the conditions and the limits—both discursive and institutional—within which reality is perceived, understood, and thus, lived. Which is to say, to transform ourselves and the social reality we are in, we have to address the discourses that structure it, since they represent "ways of seeing, saying, and doing."[2] This approach allows the development of a dynamic that addresses the questions of why things are the way they are, and how they got to be that way, and helps to develop concrete possibilities for unlearning domination and work for transformation. This process is one constituted in struggle wherein the diversity of power tensions relative to questions of class, gender, race, ethnicity, and religion get articulated.

By defining pedagogical practices in this work, I showed their unavoidable political dimension by conceptualizing them as deliberate interventions in the constitution of knowledge, subjectivites, and social relations.[3] This particular discursive construction links pedagogy to democracy as its necessary theoretical and ethical referent. That is, by moving pedagogy away from the dominant discourse of methods and 'how to' recipes, we enter a discourse that addresses wider social relations and power struggles. In chapter two, I addressed democratic theory as a language, a particular communicative construction, exploring the specific radical possibilities it offers for the wider struggle of social change. In doing so, I moved away from the traditional liberal discourse of consensus to explore the emancipatory possibilities of a radical democratic discourse that takes into account a much needed politics of difference. In the third chapter, I engaged in an analysis of public spheres as utopian spaces for democratic pedagogical practices within the particular emancipatory possibilities offered by feminist discourse. The particular focus of this analysis was organized around the Mothers' movement in Argentina. In the fourth chapter, I showed how the Mothers' movement continues to constitute an active counterpublic sphere. Their collective struggle during these past years and in the present is a clear example of this.

In the fifth chapter, I extended my analysis of the interplay of pedagogy, feminism, democracy, and discourse to apply it to the rethinking of the pedagogical practices within the university setting. In this chapter, in particular, my aim was to stress the operative dimension of critical pedagogy.

In all five chapters, there has been a shifting interplay of the terms pedagogy, democracy, and discourse in an attempt to show the formative effect of discourses, both in their discursive and material dimensions, the pedagogical moments within them, and the necessity for democracy to provide a framework within power struggles in order to offer an emancipatory possibility against oppressive hegemonic social forms. In this way, I have engaged dominant discourses, like the liberal discourse, and I have worked with counterdiscourses, like radical democracy or critical pedagogy. In the struggle of discourses, similar words take a different meaning in terms of the positions from which they are used. My stand is to frame these positions, which are inscribed in the practices of class, gender, race, and others struggles, within a paradigm of emancipation. In this way, while recognizing material and structural forces, I tried to develop a sense of agency by both engaging in readings that articulate a politics of difference and uncovering practices, like the ones of the Mothers' movement in Argentina, that overflow oppressive representations.

Throughout this work I remapped the boundaries between pedagogy, feminism, democracy and discourse. In re-writing this new space, I have been mainly concerned with the articulation of a politics of difference. In doing so, I looked especially at the possibilities offered by the category public sphere as the place in which to engage in deliberation and decisionmaking.

Some Notes on New Research Directions and Challenges

Social Movements, Counter-public Spheres and the Mothers

The current democratic trend shows the presence of social movements as constituting the means for articulation of public concerns and, at the same time, a more viable way of actual participation and action within today's progressive formalization of democracy. The concrete configuration of the Mothers' movement in Argentina could work as a specific space to explore further the issue of the political subject which these kinds of movements enable and construct. The inquiry would be to search for the discursive elements around which the subject is enacted, and then analyze the possibilities this subject displays in collectively resisting and subverting contemporary neoconservative political tendencies to coopt his or her action.

The particularity of the Mothers' movement is that they offer a political discourse substantially articulated around ethical terms. They state, for example:

> Our goal is different from the one we would pursue belonging to a political party . . . Reaching our goal is going to take many years, we want to create in the young people the consciousness of something new, different. Today *peronistas, radicales* [political parties in Argentina], and else have no worth. Something new has to be born, with ethics, with solidarity; we have projects of a different life for young people . . . On one occasion, we were criticized harshly because of our resistance to integrate with a political party. We answered with an editorial article in the Mothers' paper entitled "The essence of our struggle" where we explained that it was worth more to be ethical, to be honest, not like today . . . Somebody would ask how this could be done. We say we have to start from the wombs . . . Children should be raised in solidarity, in honesty. One day a political party will have to be born with these foundations, . . . it will make of this country something different, but in the meantime . . .

This approach constitutes a complex problematic since the current realm of politics is still very much built within the terms of a formal way of negotiation which responds to a party politics structure. An ethical political discourse and, at the same time, a successful political action are still a challenge to be faced.

The Operative Dimension of Critical Pedagogy

One aspect to explore further, possibly through action-research, is the conception of the class as a site of conflict where a critical pedagogical practice constitutes an ongoing process that redefines itself constantly, taking into account both personal and social investments, and the power tensions around which they develop.

• What are the theoretical constructions that permeate/enact the practices in the classroom without the teacher's awareness? This would mean revising and critically reconstructing the work of the teacher in order to uncover the representations, conceptualizations and meanings that she/he gives to her/his practice. This approach presupposes that most of the time there is a contradiction between purposes and action, between goals pursued according to a critical perspective and the actual practices enacted in the classroom. There is also the presupposition that the meanings and representations the teacher holds as a whole constitute layers coming from a variety of constructions. These layers have progressively lost their connection with their theoretical and socio-historical origins and, in the present, form part of a common sense which, in terms of its contradictory heterogeneity, interferes with any practice the teacher intends to develop.

- Departing from the assumption that experience is structured through language, how to approach the study of language in the classroom? How to engage students' experiences in terms of the language they use? What kind of language should structure the teacher's practice within critical pedagogy's perspective?

These are only a few inquiries, among the unending realm of possibilities that critical pedagogy offers to engage everyday life, that would provide substantial elements for reflection, constructing and reconstructing more liberatory pedagogical practices.

NOTES

INTRODUCTION

1. Linda Alcoff, "Cultural Feminism Versus Post-Structuralism: The Identity Crisis in Feminist Theory," *Signs, 13* (Spring 1988), 433.

2. Peter McLaren, *Life in Schools: An Introduction to Critical Pedagogy in the Foundations of Education* (Longman, New York & London: 1989), ix.

3. Henry Giroux, *Teachers as Intellectuals: Toward a Critical Pedagogy of Learning* (Bergin & Garvey Publications, Massachusetts: 1988).

4. Henry Giroux, *Border Crossing: Cultural Workers and the Politics of Education* (Routledge, New York: 1992), 2.

CHAPTER 1

1. Henry Giroux, *Border Crossings: Cultural Workers and the Politics of Education* (Routledge, New York and London: 1992), 2.

2. Related to this question of the need of educational theory to engage other theoretical fields see: Henry Giroux, ed. *Postmodernism, Feminism, and Cultural Politics: Redrawing Educational Boundaries* (State University of New York Press, Albany: 1992); Henry Giroux, *Curriculum Discourse as Postmodernist Critical Practice* (Deakin University Press, Geelong: 1990); Cary Nelson, ed., *Theory in the Classroom* (University of Illinois Press, Urbana and Chicago: 1986); bell hooks, *Talking Back* (South End Press, Boston: 1989); Henry Giroux, Roger Simon and Contributors, *Popular Culture: Schooling and Everyday Life* (Bergin and Garvey, Massachusetts: 1989); Lawrence Grossberg, Cary Nelson, Paula Treichler, eds., *Cultural Studies* (Routledge, New York: 1992); Chandra Mohanty, Ann Russo, Lourdes Torres, eds., *Third World Women and the Politics of Feminism* (Indiana University Press, Bloomington and Indianapolis: 1991); Gayatri Spivak, *In Other Worlds: Essays in Cultural Politics* (Routledge, New York and London: 1988); Henry Giroux and Peter McLaren, eds., *Critical Pedagogy, the State, and Cultural Struggle* (State University of New York Press, Albany: 1989); David Trend, *Beyond Resistance: Cultural Work and Education* (Forthcoming).

3. Roger Simon, *Teaching Against the Grain: Essays for a Pedagogy of Possiblity* (Bergin and Garvey Press, New York: 1992).

4. For an example of analysis and work done on critical reproduction theory see: Kathleen Weiler, *Women Teaching for Change: Gender, Class, and Power* (Bergin and Garvey Press, Massachusetts: 1988); Henry Giroux, "Theories of Reproduction and Resistance in the New Sociology of Education: A Critical Analysis," *Harvard Educational Review, 53* (1983), 257–93; Jean Anyon, "Social Class and the Hidden Curriculum of Work," *Journal of Education, 162(2)* (1980), 67–92; "Social Class and School Knowledge," *Curriculum Inquiry, 11(1)* (1981), 3–42; Henry Giroux, *Ideology, Culture and the Process of Schooling* (Temple University Press, Philadelphia: 1981); Stanley Aronowitz and Henry Giroux, *Education Under Siege: The Conservative, Liberal, and Radical Debate over Schooling* (Bergin and Garvey, Massachusetts: 1985).

5. Stanley Aronowitz and Henry Giroux, "Reproduction and Resistance in Radical Theories of Schooling," in *Education Under Siege*, 69–114.

6. Louis Althusser, "Ideology and the Ideological State Apparatuses," in *Lenin and Philosophy, and Other Essays*, trans. Bev Brewster (Monthly Review Press, New York: 1971); Samuel Bowles and Herbert Gintis, *Schooling in Capitalist America* (Basic Books, New York: 1976); C. Baudelot and R. Establet, *L'Ecole Capitaliste en France* (Francois Maspero, Paris: 1971).

7. Stanley Aronowitz and Henry Giroux, *Education Under Siege*, 75.

8. Pierre Bourdieu and Jean-Claude Passeron, *Reproduction in Education, Society, and Culture* (Sage Publications, London and Beverly Hills: 1977).

9. Stanley Aronowitz and Henry Giroux, *Education Under Siege*, 82.

10. Michael Apple, *Ideology and Curriculum* (Routledge and Kegan Paul, London and Boston: 1979). This was among the first books along these lines of thinking translated into Spanish. It had a profound effect on the educational theory developed in Argentina during the beginning of the democratic period in 1984.

11. See Stanley Aronowitz and Henry Giroux, "Curriculum Theory and the Language of Possibility." In *Education Under Siege*, 139–62.

12. See Kathleen Weiler, *Women Teaching for Change*, 14–18. She does an important assessment of the domination-resistance tension, providing an interesting reading of Antonio Gramsci's approach.

13. Ibid., 21.

14. Paul Willis, *Learning to Labor* (Columbia University Press, New York: 1981).

15. Stanley Aronowitz and Henry Giroux, *Education Under Siege*, 96–104.

16. His fundamental book is *Pedagogy of the Oppressed* (Harper and Row, New York: 1971). Other important examples of Paulo Freire's work are: *Education for Crit-*

ical Consciousness (Seabury Press, New York: 1973); *Pedagogy in Process: The Letters from Guinea-Bissau* (Seabury Press, New York: 1978); *The Politics of Education* (Bergin and Garvey, South Hadley, Mass.: 1985).

17. For a general analysis on critical pedagogy see: Henry Giroux, *Teachers as Intellectuals: Toward a Critical Pedagogy of Learning* Bergin and Garvey Publications, Massachusetts: 1988); *Schooling and the Struggle for Public Life: Critical Pedagogy in the Modern Age* (University of Minnesota Press, Minneapolis: 1988); Peter McLaren, *Life in Schools: An Introduction to Critical Pedagogy in the Foundations of Education* (Longman, New York and London: 1989); "On Ideology and Education: Critical Pedagogy and the Politics of Education," *Social Text, 19/20* (1988), 153–85.

18. See Henry Giroux, "Solidarity, Ethics and Possibility in Critical Education," in *Teachers as Intellectuals*, 204–22.

19. Peter McLaren, *Life in Schools*, 160.

20. For a more extensive discussion on the main categories and conceptualizations of critical pedagogy see: Henry Giroux, "Critical Pedagogy, Cultural Politics, and the Discourse of Experience," and "Teachers as Transformative Intellectuals," in *Teachers as Intellectuals*, 86–107, 121–28; Peter McLaren, "Critical Pedagogy: A Look at the Major Concepts," in *Life in Schools*, 166–91.

21. On the question of cultural workers' inclusion in a broader conceptualization of pedagogical practices see: Roger Simon, "Teachers as Cultural Workers," in *Teaching Against the Grain*; David Trend, *Beyond Resistance*.

22. Roger Simon, "For a Pedagogy of Possibility," *Critical Pedagogy Networker, 1* (1988), 2.

23. Ibid., 2.

24. Ibid., 2. See also Henry Giroux, *Teachers as Intellectuals*; David Trend, *Beyond Resistance*.

25. Roger Simon, *Teaching Against the Grain*, 76–78.

26. Ibid., 76–77.

27. Ibid., 76.

28. Henry Giroux, *Border Crossings*, 242.

29. Ibid., 246.

30. Ibid., 240.

31. David Trend, *Beyond Resistance*, 41–42.

32. For a brief overview of some work on feminist pedagogy see: Margo Culley and Catherine Portugues, eds., *Gendered Subjects: The Dynamics of Feminist Teaching*

(Routledge and Kegan Paul, Boston, London, Melbourne and Henley: 1985); Susan Gabriel and Isaiah Smithson, eds., *Gender in the Classroom, Power and Pedagogy* (Urbana: University of Illinois Press, 1990); bell hooks, *Talking Back*; Dale Bauer, "The Other 'F' Word: The Feminist in the Classroom," *College English, 52(4)* (1990), 385–96; Linda Brodkey, "On the Subjects of Class and Gender in "The Literacy Letters,'" *College English, 51(2)* (1989), 125–41; Nell Noddings, *Caring: A Feminine Approach to Ethics and Moral Education* (University of California Press, Berkeley: 1984); Pamela Annas, "Style as Politics: A Feminist Approach to the Teaching of Writing," *College English, 47(4)* (1985), 360–71; Magda Lewis and Roger Simon, "A Discourse not Intended for Her: Learning and Teaching within Patriarchy," *Harvard Educational Review, 56(4)* (1986), 457–72; Jennifer Gore, *The Struggle for Pedagogies: Critical and Feminist Discourses as Regimes of Truth* (Routledge, New York: 1993).

33. Maria Lugones and Elizabeth Spelman, "Have we got a Theory for you! Feminist Theory, Cultural Imperialism and the Demand of the Woman's Voice," *Women's Studies International Forum, 6(6)* (1983), 573–81; Maria Lugones, "Playfulness, 'World'-travelling and Loving Perception," *Hypatia 2(2)* (1987), 3–19.

34. Henry Giroux, *Teachers as Intellectuals*, 119.

35. Mikhail Bakhtin, *The Dialogic Imagination*, trans. Caryl Emerson and Michael Holquist (University of Texas Press, Austin: 1981).

36. For further discussion on this issue see: Anthony Giddens, *Central Problems in Social Theory: Action, Structure and Contradiction in Social Analysis* (University of California Press, Berkeley and Los Angeles: 1979).

37. Gayatri Spivak, *In Other Worlds*, 77–78.

38. Maria Lugones and Elizabeth Spelman, "Have We Got a Theory for You!," 578.

39. Gayatri Spivak, *In Other Worlds*, 204. Paraphrasing Spivak, a subaltern subject-effect is conceptualized as a phenomenon where an operating subject emerges from the different configurations that a context of multiple interwoven "strands," such as politics, ideology, economics, sexuality, and language—also multiples in themselves—take in the ongoing process of contesting and subverting the dominant paradigm. The different configurations of these strands, the result of a multiplicity of conditions, have as an effect the emergence of a subject, an operating one, which is also seen as cause according to the requirements of what Spivak calls a "homogenist deliberative consciousness." Spivak states that, contrary to her conceptualization, imperialist texts situate "a will as the sovereign cause when it is no more than an effect of the subaltern subject-effect, itself produced by . . . particular conjunctures" (pp. 204–5). I find Spivak's conceptualization very empowering in the sense that she works with difference, produced within power relations, rather than with identity, enriching in this way the process of ongoing contestation in the terrain of current cultural practices. Furthermore, by arguing for a conception of the subject as both cause-effect, she problematizes binary oppositions and contests the tendency to see dominant "will" as cause and the subaltern

one as effect. Both are deconstructed and seen as merged in a complex process where cause-effect cannot be separated and assigned exclusively to the dominant or subaltern-subject.

40. Maria Lugones and Elizabeth Spelman, "Have We Got a Theory for You!," 576.

41. Ibid., 581–83.

42. Gayatri Spivak, *In Other Worlds*, 89; Maria Lugones, "Playfulness, 'World'-travelling, and Loving Perception," 574.

43. Maria Lugones and Elizabeth Spelman, "Have We Got a Theory for You!," 573.

44. Ibid., 573.

45. Ibid., 574.

46. Mikhail Bakhtin, *The Dialogic Imagination*; Richard Quantz and Terence O'Connor, "Writing Critical Ethnography: Dialogue, Multivoicedness, and Carnival in Cultural Texts," *Educational Theory, 38(1)* (1988), 95–109.

47. L. S. Vygotsky, *Mind in Society. The Development of Higher Psychological Processes* (Harvard University Press, Cambridge and London: 1978).

48. Maria Lugones and Elizabeth Spelman, "Have We Got a Theory for You!," 574.

49. Ibid., 578.

50. Ibid., 578.

51. Ibid., 578–79.

52. Ibid., 579.

53. Ibid., 579

54. Gayatri Spivak, *In Other Worlds*, x.

55. Maria Lugones and Elizabeth Spelman, "Have We Got a Theory for You!," 579.

56. Maria Lugones, "Playfulness, 'World'-travelling, and Loving Perception," 17.

57. Henry Giroux, "Postmodernism as Border Pedagogy: Redefining the Boundaries of Race and Ethnicity," in *Postmodernism, Feminism and Cultural Politics*, 217–56.

58. Signithia Fordham, "Racelessness as a Factor in Black Students' School Success: Pragmatic Strategy or Pyrric Victory?," *Harvard Educational Review, 58(1)* (1988), 54–84.

59. Henry Giroux, *Border Crossings*, 174.

60. Maria Lugones, "Playfulness, 'World'-travelling, and Loving Perception," 8.

61. Maria Lugones and Elizabeth Spelman, "Have We Got a Theory for You!," 577.

62. On the question of reading and writing see: Paulo Freire, "The Importance of the Act of Reading," *Journal of Education, 165(1)* (1983), 5–11; Robert Scholes, *Textual Power: Literary Theory and the Teaching of English* (Yale University Press, New Haven and London: 1985).

63. Maria Lugones, "Playfulness, 'World'-travelling and Loving Perception," 11.

64. Magda Lewis and Roger Simon, "A Discourse not Intended for Her."

CHAPTER 2

1. Jhon Keane, *Democracy and Civil Society* (Verso, London and New York: 1988), 10.

2. About the problematic facing Latin America, see: Vanilda Paiva, Educación, *Bienestar Social y Trabajo* (Coquena Grupo Editor, Buenos Aires: 1992); Norma Paviglianiti, *Neoconservadurismo y Educación* (Coquena Grupo Editor, Buenos Aires: 1991).

3. Document of the Ministry of Culture and Education, "New School: More and better education for everybody," May 1993.

4. Examples of work on this issue include: Henry A. Giroux, *Teachers as Intellectuals* (Bergin and Garvey, Massachusetts: 1988); *Schooling and the Struggle for Public Life* (University of Minnesota Press, Minneapolis: 1988); Roger Simon, "For a Pedagogy of Possibility." *Critical Pedagogy Networker 1(1)* (1988), 1–4; Kathleen Weiler, *Women Teaching for Change* (Bergin and Garvey, Massachusetts: 1988); Margo Culley and Catherine Portugues, eds., *Gendered Subjects: The Dynamics of Feminist Teaching* (Routledge and Kegan Paul, New York: 1985); Dale Bauer, "The Other 'F' Word: The Feminist in the Classroom," *College English 51(4)* (1990), 885–96; Henry A. Giroux and Peter L. McLaren, *Between Borders. Pedagogy and the Politics of Cultural Studies* (Routledge, New York: 1994).

5. Kathy E. Ferguson, *The Feminist Case Against Bureaucracy* (Temple University Press, Philadelphia: 1984), 154.

6. This issue is taken up in detail in Ernesto Laclau and Chantal Mouffe, *Hegemony and Socialist Strategy* (Verso, London and New York: 1985); Kathy Ferguson, *The Feminist Case Against Bureaucracy*.

7. Kathy Ferguson, *The Feminist Case Against Bureaucracy*; bell hooks, *Talking Back: Thinking Feminist, Thinking Black* (South End Press, Boston: 1989); Gloria

Anzaldua, ed., *Making Face, Making Soul: Haciendo Caras* (San Francisco: an Aunt Lute Foundation book).

8. For an important discussion on this topic see: Helen Cixous and Catherine Clement, *The Newly Born Woman* (University of Minnesota Press, Minneapolis: 1986).

9. Samuel Bowles and Herbert Gintis, *Democracy and Capitalism: Property, Community, and the Contradictions of Modern Social Thought* (Basic Books, New York: 1987), 161.

10. Stuart Hall and David Held, "Citizens and Citizenship" in *New Times: The Changing Face of Politics in the 1990s*. Stuart Hall and Martin Jacques, eds. (Verso, London and New York: 1990), 173–88.

11. Bowles and Gintis, *Democracy and Capitalism*, 153.

12. Ibid., 152–54.

13. Ibid., 153.

14. Richard Quantz and Terry O'Connor, "Writing critical ethnography: Dialogue, Multivoicedness, and Carnival in Cultural Texts," *Educational Theory 38(1)*, 95–109.

15. Bowles and Gintis, *Democracy and Capitalism*, 157–58.

16. Ibid.

17. Michel Foucault, *The History of Sexuality. Volume I: An Introduction*, trans. Robert Hurley (Vintage Books, New York: 1980), 93.

18. Edward Said, *Orientalism* (Vintage Books, New York: 1979).

19. Antonio Gramsci, *Selections From the Prison Notebooks*, ed. and trans. Quintin Hoare and Geoffrey Newell Smith (International Publishers, New York: 1971).

20. Raymond Williams, *Marxism and Literature* (Oxford University Press, Oxford: 1977).

21. Foucault, *The History of Sexuality. Volume 1*.

22. Ibid.

23. Bowles and Gintis, *Democracy and Capitalism*, 97.

24. Ibid., 97.

25. Ibid., 10.

26. Ibid., 11.

27. Laclau and Mouffe, *Hegemony and Socialist Strategy*, 155.

28. Chantal Mouffe, "Radical Democracy or Liberal Democracy?," *Socialist Review 20(2)* (April–June 1990), 57–66.

29. Laclau and Mouffe, *Hegemony and Socialist Strategy*, 63.

30. Bowles and Gintis, *Democracy and Capitalism*, 4.

31. Ibid., 4.

32. For an excellent discussion on this issue see: Roger Simon, *Teaching Against the Grain* (Bergin & Garvey, New York: 1992).

33. Mouffe, "Radical Democracy or Liberal Democracy," 58.

34. Bowles and Gintis, *Democracy and Capitalism*, 16–7.

35. On this issue see Iris M. Young, *Justice and the Politics of Difference* (Princeton University Press, Princeton: 1990).

36. Bowles and Gintis, *Democracy and Capitalism*, 100.

37. Ibid., 17.

38. Ibid., 17.

39. Ibid., 127.

40. Ibid., 127.

41. For a thorough discussion of the liberal distinction of public and private spheres see: Nancy Fraser, "What's Critical about Critical Theory? The Case of Habermas and Gender" in *Unruly Practices: Power, Discourse and Gender in Contemporary Social Theory* (University of Minnesota Press, Minneapolis: 1989), 113–43; Nancy Fraser, "Rethinking the Public Sphere: A Contribution to the Critique of Actually Existing Democracy" in *Between Borders. Pedagogy and the Politics of Cultural Studies*; Carole Pateman, "Feminist Critiques of the Public/Private Dichotomy" in *The Disorder of Women* (Stanford University Press, Stanford: 1989), 118–40; Kathy Ferguson, *The Feminist Case Against Bureaucracy*; Michael Walzer, "Liberalism and the Art of Separation," *Political Theory 12* (1984), 314–20; Iris Young, *Justice and the Politics of Difference*.

42. For a particularly interesting discussion on this perspective see: Iris Young, "The Ideal of Impartiality and the Civic Public" in *Justice and the Politics of Difference*, 96–121.

43. Bowles and Gintis, *Democracy and Capitalism*, 16.

44. Ibid., 17–18.

45. Carole Pateman, "The Fraternal Social Contract" in *The Disorder of Women*, 33–57. She offers an important critique of the liberal dichotomies, pointing out how current studies still ignore that underneath the separations and splits the opposition between the sexes is also represented.

46. On the question of women's bodies and the private/public split, see Iris Young, *Justice and the Politics of Difference*, 107–8; Carole Pateman, *The Disorder of Women*.

47. Carole Pateman, *The Disorder of Women*.

48. Jean Bethke Elshtain, *Public Man, Private Woman: Women in Social and Political Thought* (Princeton University Press, Princeton: 1989).

49. David Held, *Models of Democracy* (Stanford University Press, Stanford: 1987), 292.

50. Ibid., 293.

51. For a wider discussion on the issues of accountability, democratic decision-making, and public discussion, see: Stanley Aronowitz, "Marxism and Democracy" in *The Crisis in Historical Materialism* (University of Minnesota Press, Minneapolis: 1990), 299–301; Iris Young, "Insurgency and the Welfare Capitalist Society" in *Justice and the Politics of Difference*, 66–95.

52. For a more thorough discussion of the problematic of bureaucratization and the lack of constituency's representation, see: Stanley Aronowitz, "Marxism and Democracy" in *The Crisis in Historical Materialism*. Kathy Ferguson, in *The Feminist Case Against Bureaucracy*, offers a particularly powerful critical discussion of bureaucratic power within organizations, suggesting an alternative approach that draws from a specifically feminist discourse.

53. Held, *Models of Democracy*, 293.

54. Ibid., 293.

55. Bowles and Gintis, *Democracy and Capitalism*, 66–67.

56. Ibid., 148.

57. Iris Young, *Justice and the Politics of Difference*, 121.

58. Ibid., 121.

CHAPTER 3

1. Rita Felski, *Beyond Feminist Aesthetics: Feminist Literature and Social Change* (Harvard University Press, Cambridge: 1989), 12.

2. Jean B. Elshtain, *Public Man, Private Woman: Women in Social and Political Thought* (Princeton University Press, Princeton: 1989).

3. Close to this line of thought, Nancy Fraser develops a brilliant analysis of Habermas's account of the relations between public and private institutions in classical capitalist societies in terms of the roles that mediate them. She argues that these roles, such as worker, consumer, and citizen, are gendered ones. Therefore, the links between private and public institutions "are forged in the medium of masculine gender identity rather than, as Habermas has it, in the medium of a gender-neutral power. Or, if the

medium of exchange here is power, then the power in question is masculine power: it is power as the expression of masculinity." Nancy Fraser, "What's Critical about Critical Theory? The Case of Habermas and Gender" in *Unruly Practices: Power, Discourse and Gender in Contemporary Social Theory* (University of Minnesota Press, Minneapolis: 1989), 123.

4. Judy Butler, *Gender Trouble* (Routledge, New York: 1988), 24.

5. Ibid., 24.

6. María del Carmen Feijoo, "The Challenge of Constructing Civil Peace: Women and Democracy in Argentina" in *The Women's Movement in Latin America*, Jane Jaquette, ed. (Unwin Hyman, Boston: 1989), 75.

7. Gloria Bonder, "The Study of Politics from the Standpoint of Women," *International Social-Sciences Journal, 35(4)* (1983), 569–83.

8. Feijoo, "The Challenge of Constructing Civil Peace," 77.

9. Jean P. Bousquet, *Las Locas de la Plaza de Mayo* (El Cid Editor, Buenos Aires: 1983).

10. Feijoo, "The Challenge of Constructing Civil Peace," 78.

11. Ibid., 77.

12. Jane Jaquette, ed., *The Women's Movement in Latin America* (Unwin Hyman, Boston: 1989).

13. Elshtain, *Public Man, Private Woman*, 300.

14. Ibid., 304.

15. Ibid., 306–10, 323–25.

16. Ibid., 305.

17. Nancy Fraser, "Rethinking the Public Sphere: A Contribution to the Critique of Actually Existing Democracy," *Social Text, 25/6* (1990), 70.

18. Elshtain, *Public Man, Private Woman*, 323–28.

19. Ibid., 331.

20. Ibid., 337.

21. Ibid., 345.

22. Ibid., 346.

23. Butler, *Gender Trouble*, 2.

24. Teresa De Lauretis, *Technologies of Gender: Essays on Theory, Film, and Fiction* (Indiana University Press, Bloomington, Indianapolis: 1987), 9. For an inter-

esting comparative analysis on women's discourse and the sophists' marginalization within philosophical thought, see Susan Jarratt, "The First Sophists and Feminism: Discourses of the 'Other,'" *Hypatia, 5(1)* (1989), 27–41.

25. Gayatri C. Spivak, *In Other Worlds: Essays in Cultural Politics* (Routledge, New York, London: 1988); Jarratt, "The First Sophists and Feminism: Discourses of the 'Other'"; De Lauretis, *Technologies of Gender.*

26. De Lauretis, *Technologies of Gender*, 10.

27. Ibid., 2.

28. Ibid., 2.

29. Gayatri Spivak quoted in Jarratt, "The First Sophists and Feminism," 29.

30. Richard Johnson, "What is Cultural Studies Anyway," *Anglistica, 26(1–2)* (1983), 49.

31. Sandra Morgen and Ann Bookman, eds., *Women and the Politics of Empowerment* (Temple University Press, Philadelphia: 1988).

32. Bonder, "The Study of Politics from the Standpoint of Women," 580.

33. Feijoo, "The Challenge of Constructing Civil Peace," 79.

34. Bonder, "The Study of Politics from the Standpoint of Women," 570.

35. The concept of 'doer' is taken from Judy Butler, *Gender Trouble*, 25.

36. The expression 'non-identity' comes from Rebeca Chopp, *The Praxis of Suffering: An Interpretation of Liberation and Political Theologies* (Orbis Books, Maryknoll: 1986).

37. This part of the text draws extensively on Gloria Bonder's analysis of the woman/mother equivalence in the public statements of dictatorial regimes, 578–82.

38. I owe the expression 'unlearn oppression' to a personal conversation on the topic with Dr. Henry A. Giroux.

39. Feijoo, "The Challenge of Constructing Civil Peace," 78.

40. Nancy Fraser, "Rethinking the Public Sphere," 57.

41. Ibid., 57.

42. Ibid., 57.

43. Ibid., 62.

44. Iris M. Young, *Justice and the Politics of Difference* (Princeton University Press, Princeton: 1990), 98.

45. Fraser, "Rethinking the Public Sphere," 68.

46. Ibid., 75.

47. Young, *Justice and the Politics of Difference*, 184.

48. Fraser, "Rethinking the Public Sphere," 62.

49. Ibid., 71.

50. Ibid., 71.

51. Young, *Justice and the Politics of Difference*, 120.

52. Fraser, "Rethinking the Public Sphere," 73.

53. De Lauretis, *Technologies of Gender*, 10.

CHAPTER 4

1. The Military coup took place in March 1976.

2. Neuquén is a province in the south of Argentina, placed on the North part of Patagonia region and bordering with Chile.

3. Omar Carrasco was a young man (eighteen years old) complying with the Obligatory Military Service in an Army base in Zapala city, province of Neuquén. In March 1994, he was reported as having escaped the base after only a few days of his registration there. He was then found dead in the base. He had been beaten to death. The Carrasco case was taken by Civil Courts. The trial was shown by public TV channels. By the end of 1995, two conscripts and two officials were convicted. Their lawyers have appealed the sentence. As a consequence of this, the Military Service became a fundamental topic of general discussion. A new law has been elaborated that makes Military Service optional.

4. CONADEP. It was organized in 1984 by the first constitutional president Raúl Alfonsin after the Military regime. Its purpose was to investigate the disappearances which took place under that regime.

CHAPTER 5

1. Diane Macdonell, *Theories of Discourse: An Introduction* (Basil Blackwell, New York: 1986), 51.

2. Roger Simon, *Teaching Against the Grain: Essays for a Pedagogy of Possibility* (Bergin and Garvey Press, New York: 1992), 158.

3. Peter McLaren, "Schooling the Postmodern Body: Critical Pedagogy and the Politics of Enfleshment" in *Postmodernism, Feminism and Cultural Politics: Redrawing Educational Boundaries*, Henry Giroux, ed. (State University of New York, Albany: 1991), 173.

4. Henry Giroux, *Curriculum Discourse as Postmodernist Critical Practice* (Deakin University Press, Geelong: 1990).

5. For a critical analysis on those lines of thought see: Roger Simon, *Teaching Against the Grain*; Henry Giroux, "Language, Difference, and Curriculum Theory: Beyond the Politics of Clarity," in *Theory into Practice* (In Press).

6. Henry Giroux, "Cultural Studies, Resisting Difference, and the Return of Critical Pedagogy" in *Border Crossing: Cultural Workers and the Politics of Education* (Routledge, New York: 1992).

7. Henry Giroux, *Border Crossing*, 97.

8. Donna Haraway, "Situated Knowledges: The Science Question in Feminism and the Privilege of Partial Perspective," *Feminist Studies, 14(3)* (1989).

9. Michel Foucault, *Power and Knowledge*, Colin Gordon, ed., trans. by Colin Gordon, Leo Marshall, John Mapham, and Kate Soper (Pantheon Books, New York: 1977).

10. This problematic has been detected in diverse Latin American universities and is discussed by Alicia de Alba in her book *Curriculum: Crisis, Mito y Perspectivas* (Universidad Autonoma de Mexico, Mexico: 1991).

11. Linda Alcoff, "Cultrual Feminism Versus Post-Structuralism: The Identity Crisis in Feminist Theory," *Signs, 13* (Spring 1988), 405–37.

12. Michel Foucault, *The Archaeology of Knowledge* (Tavistock, London: 1972).

13. For an important analysis on this topic see: Roger Simon, "The Fear of Theory" in *Teaching Against the Grain*, 147–87.

14. Magda Lewis and Roger Simon, "A Discourse not Intended for Her," 469.

15. Peter McLaren, "Critical Pedagogy: Constructing an arch of social dreaming and a doorway to hope," *Journal of Education, 173(1)* (1991), 10.

16. Ibid., 27.

17. See Roger Simon, "For a Pedagogy of Possibility," 2.

18. See Joe L. Kincheloe, *Teachers as researchers: Qualitative Inquiry as a path to empowerment* (The Falmer Press, London: 1991).

19. See Thomas Popkewitz, *Paradigma e ideología en investigación educativa: Las funciones sociales del intelectual* (Mondadori, Madrid: 1992).

20. See Henry Giroux, *Teachers as Intellectuals.*

21. For further analysis see Henry Giroux, *Theory and Resistance in Education: A Pedagogy for the Opposition* (Bergin and Garvey, South Hadley, Mass.: 1983), Chapter 4.

22. Robert Scholes, *Textual Power*, 15–16.

23. Ibid., 20.

24. Paula Treichler, "Teaching Feminist Theory" in *Theory in the Classroom*, Cary Nelson, ed. (University of Illinois Press, Urbana and Chicago: 1986), 57–128.

25. Jill Eichhorn, Sara Farris, Karen Hayes, Adriana Hernández, Susan Jarratt, Karen Powers-Stubbs, and Marian Sciachitano, "A Symposium on Feminist Experiences in the Composition Classroom," *College Composition and Communication 43(3)* (1992), 297–322.

26. Ibid., 318.

27. Ibid., 317.

28. Ibid., 317.

CHAPTER 6

1. Diane Macdonell, *Theories of Discourse*, 49.

2. Roger Simon, *Teaching Against the Grain*, 117.

3. Henry Giroux, *Border Crossing*, 2; Roger Simon, "For a Pedagogy of Possibility," *Critical Pedagogy Networker, 1* (1988), 2.

BIBLIOGRAPHY

Alcoff, Linda. (1988). "Cultural Feminism Versus Post-Structuralism: The Identity Crisis in Feminist Theory." *Signs, 13*, 405–436.

Althusser, Louis. (1971). *Ideology and the Ideological State Apparatuses. In Lenin and Philosophy, and Other Essays*, trans. Bev Brewster. New York: Monthly Review Press.

Annas, Pamela. (1985). "Style as Politics: A Feminist Approach to the Teaching of Writing." *College English, 47(4)*, 360–71.

Anyon, Jean. (1980). "Social Class and the Hidden Curriculum of Work." *Journal of Education, 162(2)*, 67–92.

———. (1981). "Social Class and School Knowledges." *Curriculum Inquiry, 11(1)*, 3–42.

Anzaldua, Gloria. (1990). *Making Face: Making Soul. Haciendo Caras*. San Francisco: an Aunt Lute Foundation book.

Apple, Michael. (1979). *Ideology and Curriculum*. London & Boston: Routledge and Kegan Paul.

Aronowitz, Stanley, Giroux, Henry. (1985). *Education Under Siege: The Conservative, Liberal, and Radical Debate Over Schooling*. Massachusetts: Bergin and Garvey.

Aronowitz, Stanley. (1990). *The Crisis in Historical Materialism*. Minneapolis: University of Minnesota Press.

Bakhtin, Mikhail. (1981). *The Dialogic Imagination*, trans. Caryl Emerson and Michael Holquist. Austin: University of Texas Press.

Baudelot, C., Establet, R. (1971). *L'Ecole Capitaliste en France*. Paris: Francois Maspero.

Bauer, Dale. (1990). "The Other 'F' Word: The Feminist in the Classroom." *College English, 52(4)*, 385–96.

Bonder, Gloria. (1983). "The Study of Politics from the Standpoint of Women." *International Social Sciences Journal, 35(4)*, 569–83.

Bourdieu, Pierre, Passeron, Jean-Claude. (1977). *Reproduction in Education, Society, and Culture*. London and Beverly Hills: Sage Publications.

Bousquet, Jean. (1983). *Las Locas de la Plaza de Mayo*. Buenos Aires: El Cid Editor.

Bowles, Samuel, Gintis, Herbert. (1976). *Schooling in Capitalist America*. New York: Basic Books.

———. (1987). *Democracy and Capitalism: Property, Community, and the Contradictions of Modern Social Thought*. New York: Basic Books.

Brady, Jeane, Hernández, Adriana. (1993). "Feminist Literacies: Toward Emancipatory Possibilities of Solidarity." *Critical Literacy: Politics, Praxis, and the Postmodern*, Colin Lankshear and Peter McLaren, eds. Albany: State University of New York Press.

Brodkey, Linda. (1989). "On the Subjects of Class and Gender in 'The Literacy Letter.'" *College English, 51(2)*, 125–41.

Butler, Judith. (1988). *Gender Trouble*. New York: Routledge.

Chopp, Rebeca. (1986). *The Praxis of Suffering: An Interpretation of Liberation and Political Theologies*. Maryknoll: Orbis Books.

Cixous, Helen, Clement, Catherine. (1986). *The Newly Born Woman*. Minneapolis: University of Minnesota Press.

Culley, Margo, Portugues, Catherine, eds. (1985). *Gendered Subjects: The Dynamics of Feminist Teaching*. Boston, London, Melbourne, and Henley: Routledge and Kegan Paul.

de Alba, Alicia. (1991). *Curriculum: Crisis, Mito y Perspectivas*. Mexico: Universidad Nacional Autonoma de Mexico.

De Lauretis, Teresa. (1987). *Technologies of Gender: Essays on Theory, Film, and Fiction*. Bloomington and Indianapolis: Indiana University Press.

Document of the Ministry of Culture and Education, Argentina, "New School: More and Better Education for Everybody," May 1993.

Eichhorn, Jill, et al. (1992). "A Symposium on Feminist Experiences in the Composition Classroom." *College Composition and Communication 43(3)*, 297–98.

Elshtain, Jean Bethke. (1989). *Public Man, Private Woman: Women in Social and Political Thought*. Princeton: Princeton University Press.

Felski, Rita. (1989). *Beyond Feminist Aesthetics: Feminist Literature and Social Change*. Cambridge: Harvard University Press.

Ferguson, Kathy. (1984). *The Feminist Case Against Bureaucracy*. Philadelphia: Temple University Press.

Fordham, Signithia. (1988). "Racelessness as a Factor in Black Students' School Success: Pragmatic Strategy or Phyrric Victory?" *Harvard Educational Review, 58(1)*, 54–84.

Foucault, Michel. (1972). *The Archaeology of Knowledge*. London: Tavistock.

———. (1977). *Power and Knowledge*, edited by Colin Gordon and trans. by Colin Gordon, Leo Marshall, John Maphan, and Kate Soper. New York: Pantheon Books.

———. (1980). *The History of Sexuality. Volume 1: An Introduction*, trans. Robert Hurley. New York: Vintage Books.

Fraser, Nancy. (1989). *Unruly Practices: Power, Discourse and Gender in Contemporary Social Theory*. Minneapolis: University of Minnesota Press.

———. (1990). "Rethinking the Public Sphere: A Contribution to the Critique of Actually Existing Democracy." *Social Text, 25/6*, 56–79.

Freire, Paulo. (1971). *Pedagogy of the Oppressed*. New York: Harper and Row.

———. (1973). *Education for Critical Consciousness*. New York: Seabury Press.

———. (1978). *Pedagogy in Process: The Letters from Guinea-Bissau*. New York: Seabury Press.

———. (1983). "The Importance of the Act of Reading." *Journal of Education, 165(1)*, 5–11.

———. (1985). *The Politics of Education*. South Hadley, Massachusetts: Bergin and Garvey.

Gabriel, Susan, Smithson, Isaiah, eds. (1990). *Gender in the Classroom, Power and Pedagogy*. Urbana: University of Illinois Press.

Giddens, Anthony. (1979). *Central Problems in Social Theory: Action, Structure and Contradictions in Social Analysis*. Berkeley and Los Angeles: University of California Press.

Giroux, Henry. (1981). *Ideology, Culture and the Process of Schooling*. Philadelphia: Temple University Press.

———. (1983). "Theories of Reproduction and Resistance in the New Sociology of Education: A Critical Analysis." *Harvard Educational Review, 53*, 257–93.

———. (1983). *Theory and Resistance in Education. A Pedagogy for the Opposition*. Massachusetts: Bergin and Garvey.

———. (1988). *Teachers as Intellectuals: Toward a Critical Pedagogy of Learning*. Massachusetts: Bergin and Garvey.

————. (1988). *Schooling and the Struggle for Public Life: Critical Pedagogy in the Modern Age*. Minneapolis: University of Minnesota Press.

————, Simon, Roger, and Contributors. (1989). *Popular Culture: Schooling and Everyday Life*. Massachusetts: Bergin and Garvey.

————, McLaren, Peter, eds. (1989). *Critical Pedagogy, the State, and Cultural Struggle*. Albany: State University of New York Press.

————. (1990). *Curriculum Discourse as Postmodernist Critical Practice*. Geelong: Deakin University Press.

————, ed. (1991). *Postmodernism, Feminism, and Cultural Politics: Redrawing Educational Boundaries*. Albany: State University of New York Press.

————. (1992). *Border Crossing. Cultural Workers and the Politics of Education*. New York: Routledge.

————. (In Press). "Language, Difference, and Curriculum Theory: Beyond the Politics of Clarity." *Theory into Practice*.

————, McLaren, Peter. (1994). *Between Borders. Pedagogy and the Politics of Cultural Studies*. New York: Routledge.

Gore, Jennifer M. (1993). *The Struggle for Pedagogies: Critical and Feminist Discourses as Regimes of Truth*. New York: Routledge.

Gramsci, Antonio. (1971). *Selections from the Prison Notebook*, ed. and trans. Quintin Hoare and Geoffrey Newell Smith. New York: International Publishers.

Grossberg, Lawrence, Nelson, Cary, Treichler, Paula, eds. (1992). *Cultural Studies*. New York: Routledge.

Hall, Stuart, Held, David. (1990). "Citizens and Citizenship." In *New Times: The Changing Face of Politics in the 1990s*. London and New York: Verso.

Haraway, Donna. (1989). "Situated Knowledges: The Science Question in Feminism and the Privilege of Partial Perspective." *Feminist Studies, 14(3)*.

Held, David. (1987). *Models of Democracy*. Stanford: Stanford University Press.

Hernández, Adriana. (1989). "Feminist Theory, Plurality of Voices and Cultural Imperialism." *Philosophical Studies in Education*. Proceedings—Annual meeting of the Ohio Valley Philosophy of Education Society.

hooks, bell. (1989). *Talking Back*. Boston: South End Press.

Jaquette, Jane, ed. (1989). *The Women's Movement in Latin America*. Boston: Unwin Hymes.

Jarratt, Susan. (1989). "The First Sophists and Feminism: Discourses of the 'Other.'" *Hypatia, 5(1)*, 27–41.

Johnson, Richard. (1983). "What is Cultural Studies, Anyway?" *Anglistica, 26(1–2)*.

Kincheloe, Joe L. (1991). *Teachers as Researchers: Qualitative Inquiry a Path to Empowerment*. London: The Palmer Press.

La Belle, Thomas, Ward, Christopher. (1994). *Multiculturalism and Education. Diversity and Its Impact on Schools and Society*. Albany: State University of New York Press.

Laclau, Ernesto, Mouffe, Chantal. (1985). *Hegemony and Socialist Strategy*. London, New York: Verso.

Lewis, Magda, Simon, Roger. (1986). "A Discourse not Intended for Her: Learning and Teaching Within Patriarchy." *Harvard Educational Review, 56(4)*, 457–72.

Lugones, María, Spelman, Elizabeth. (1983). "Have We Got a Theory for You! Feminist Theory, Cultural Imperialism and the Demand of the Woman's Voice." *Women's Studies International Forum, 6(6)*, 573–81.

Lugones, María. (1987). "Playfulness, 'World'-travelling and Loving Perception." *Hypatia, 2(2)*, 3–19.

Macdonell, Diane. (1986). *Theories of Discourse: An Introduction*. New York: Basil Blackwell.

Macedo, Donaldo. (1994). *Literacies of Power, What Americans are not allowed to know*. Boulder, San Francisco and Oxford: Westview Press.

McLaren, Peter L. (1988). "On Ideology and Education: Critical Pedagogy and the Politics of Education." *Socialist Text, 19/20*, 153–85.

———. (1989). *Life in Schools: An Introduction to Critical Pedagogy in the Foundations of Education*. New York and London: Longman.

———. (1991). "Schooling the Postmodern Body: Critical Pedagogy and the Politics of Enfleshment." *Postmodernism, Feminism, and Cultural Politics*, Henry Giroux, ed. Albany: State University of New York Press.

———. (1991). "Critical Pedagogy: Constructing an Arch of Social Dreaming and a Doorway to Hope." *Journal of Education, 173(1)*, 9–34.

———. (1995). *Critical Pedagogy and Predatory Culture*. London and New York: Routledge.

———, Giarelli, James M., eds. (1995). *Critical Theory and Education Research*. Albany: State University of New York Press.

———, Lankshear, Colin, eds. (1994). *Politics of liberation. Paths from Freire*. London and New York: Routledge.

McLeod, Beverly, ed. (1994). *Language and Learning. Educating Linguistically Diverse Students*. Albany: State University of New York Press.

Mohanty, Chandra, Russo, Ann, Torres, Lourdes, eds. (1991). *Third World Women and the Politics of Feminism.* Bloomington and Indianapolis: Indiana University Press.

Morgen, Sandra, Bookman, Ann, eds. (1988). *Women and the Politics of Empowerment.* Philadelphia: Temple University Press.

Mouffe, Chantal. (1990). "Radical Democracy or Liberal Democracy?" *Socialist Review, 20(2),* 57–66.

Nelson, Cary, ed. (1986). *Theory in the Classroom.* Urbana and Chicago: University of Illinois Press.

Noddings, Nell. (1984). *Caring: A Feminine Approach to Ethics and Moral Education.* Berkeley: University of California Press.

Pateman, Carole. (1989). *The Disorder of Women.* Standford: Standford University Press.

Popkewitz, Thomas S. (1992). *Paradigma e Ideología en Investigación Educativa.* Barcelona: Mondadori.

Quantz, Richard, O'Connor, Terence. (1988). "Writing Critical Ethnography: Dialogue, Multivoicedness, and Carnival in Cultural Texts." *Educational Theory, 38(1),* 95–109.

Said, Edward. (1979). *Orientalism.* New York: Vintage Books.

Scholes, Robert. (1985). *Textual Power.* New Haven and London: Yale University Press.

Simon, Roger. (1988). "For a Pedagogy of Possibility." *Critical Pedagogy Networker, 1,* 1–4.

———. (1992). *Teaching Against the Grain: Essays for a Pedagogy of Possibility.* New York: Bergin and Garvey Press.

Spivak, Gayatri. (1988). *In Other Worlds: Essays in Cultural Politics.* New York and London: Routledge.

Trend, David. *Beyond Resistance.* (Forthcoming).

———. (1995). *The Crisis of Meaning in Culture and Education.* Minneapolis and London: University of Minnesota Press.

Vygotsky, L. S. (1978). *Mind in Society. The Development of Higher Psychological Processes.* Cambridge and London: Harvard University Press.

Walzer, Michael. (1984). "Liberalism and the Art of Separation." *Political Theory, 12,* 314–20.

Weiler, Kathleen. (1988). *Women Teaching for Change: Gender, Class, and Power.* Massachusetts: Bergin and Garvey.

Williams, John. (1994). *Classroom in Conflict. Teaching Controversial Subjects in a Diverse Society.* Albany: State University of New York Press.

Williams, Raymond. (1977). *Marxism and Literature.* Oxford: Oxford University Press.

Willis, Paul. (1981). *Learning to Labor.* New York: Columbia University Press.

Young, Iris. (1990). *Justice and the Politics of Difference.* Princeton: Princeton University Press.

INDEX

Gintis, Herbert, 9, 27–30, 33, 39–40
Giroux, Henry, 10
Gramsci, Antonia, 9, 29

Habermas, Jurgen, 55
Hall, Stuart, 27
Held, David, 27, 37–38
hooks, bell, 25

identity, 17, 19
    logic of, 56
    See also subject/ivitity

Jaquette, Jane, 46
Johnson, Richard, 51

knowledge
    common sense, 87
    school, 86–87
    students, 88

Laclau, Ernesto, 31–32
language/s
    and experience, 25–26
    and human discourse, 15
    and subjectivity, 26
    of critique and possibility, 14, 60
    of democracy, 30
    learning, 84
    See also discourse
liberalism
    and democracy, 32–36
    and the private–public split, 36–40
Lugones, María, 14–21

Mother's movement
    and collective memories, 75–77
    and counterdiscourse, 62–66
    and democratic culture, 71–73
    and political subjects, 73–75
    and the socialization of motherhood,
        66–71
    history of the, 45, 50, 52–45
Mouffe, Chantal, 33

neoconservatism, 23–24

O'Connor, Terence, 28

Paterman, Carole, 37
pedagogy
    and critical, 8, 10–11
    and cultural politics, 12–13
    and democracy, 7
    and difference, 81
    and politics, 7
    and teacher education, 85
    definition of, 11, 13
    feminist, 88–90
    pedagogical practices, 12, 53
politics
    and gender, 44, 51–53
    of difference, 7, 80–81
    of representation, 60
    See also power
power
    and pedagogy, 32
    and politics, 28–30
practice
    and pedagogy, 12
    and theory, 7, 79–80
    See also theory
    theorizing the, 14
private, 36–40, 46–48, 55–59
    definition of, 59
production, 10–11
    identity, 12
public, 36–40, 46–48, 55–59
    definition of, 59
public sphere
    and the public–private split, 39–40
    and the university, 82
    counterpublic sphere, 54
    definition of, 55
    democratic, 35
    feminist, 41, 47

Quantz, Richard, 28

school
    schooling, 8–9
    settings, 10–11
society, 33–34